T0328400

BACKSTAGE PASS

for

Trainers,
Facilitators,

and

Public Speakers

Dedicated to every person who opens doors by saying, "You can do it."

*Especially Charlie, my steady sunshine—and
Lauren, the flower of my heart.*

BACKSTAGE PASS
for
Trainers,
Facilitators,
and
Public Speakers

Your Guide to Successful Presentations

SUSAN J. JONES

CORWIN PRESS
A SAGE Publications Company
Thousand Oaks, California

For information:

Corwin Press
A Sage Publications Company
2455 Teller Road
Thousand Oaks, California 91320
www.corwinpress.com

Sage Publications Ltd.
1 Oliver's Yard
55 City Road
London EC1Y 1SP
United Kingdom

Sage Publications India Pvt. Ltd.
B-42, Panchsheel Enclave
Post Box 4109
New Delhi 110 017 India

Printed in the United States of America

Library of Congress Cataloging-in-Publication Data

Jones, Susan J.
Backstage pass for trainers, facilitators, and public speakers: Your guide to successful presentations/Susan J. Jones
    p. cm.
Includes bibliographical references and index.
ISBN 1-4129-1500-7 (cloth)
ISBN 1-4129-1501-5 (pbk)
    1. Public speaking. 2. Training. 3. Group facilitation. I. Title.
PN4129.15.J66 2006
808.5′1—dc22

                                    2005006538

This book is printed on acid-free paper.

05 06 07 10 9 8 7 6 5 4 3 2 1

Acquisitions Editor:	Faye Zucker
Editorial Assistant:	Gem Rabanera
Production Editor:	Denise Santoyo
Copy Editor:	Toni Williams
Typesetter:	C&M Digitals (P) Ltd.
Indexer:	Pamela Van Huss
Cover Designer:	Michael Dubowe

Contents

Preface   **ix**

About the Author   **xi**

Introduction   **1**

1. Preparation Precedes Success   **3**

Clear Communication: Exceeding Expectations   3

Questions and Answers   4

    Minimizing the Chance for Misunderstanding   4

    Tailoring Programs: One Size Does Not Fit All   6

    Preparing Handouts   6

    Organizing for Relaxed Delivery   8

Do's and Don'ts   8

2. Little Things Mean a Lot   **9**

Sleep for Efficiency   9

Eat for Sustained Energy   10

Dress for Success   11

Pack Light and Catch the Early Train   11

Questions and Answers   12

    Packing Checklist   12

    Sharing Book Resources   14

    Heading Off Equipment Trouble   14

    Hydration–Wet Your Whistle to Whet Your Brain   15

Do's and Don'ts   16

3. Lights, Camera, Action!   **17**

Readying the Facility   17

Materials   19

Start Before You Begin   19

Questions and Answers 20
    Crutches to Stay Calm and on Course 20
    Room Setup: The Good, the Bad, and the
       Adjustments 21
    Seating Participants for Great Results 21
    Distributing Handouts and Materials 23
    Charts, Slides, and Overheads 23
    Grand Entrances 24
Do's and Don'ts 25

4. Quick—Let 'Em Love You! **26**
Gaining Acceptance 26
Building Audience Rapport 27
    Vulnerability 27
    Establish Common Ground 27
    Friendly Is Good, Familiar Is Not 27
    Acknowledge Knowledge and Know-How 28
Working Around Personal Quirks 28
Questions and Answers 28
    Honoring Audience Expertise 29
    Increasing Visibility 30
    Changing an Audience's Point of View 30
    Agendas and Overviews 31
    Introductions and Openers 32
    Positive Communication 34
Do's and Don'ts 35

5. Put Teeth Into Your Technique **37**
Purpose Drives Process 37
Question and Answers 38
    Delivering the Main Course: Information,
       Skills, and Message 38
    Limiting Content 39
    Reflections and Connections 39
    Motivating an Audience 40
    Generating New Thinking 42
    Understanding: Taking the Road Less Traveled 42
    Nonverbal Communication 44
    Small Groups to Enliven Learning 47
    Timing Group Work 48
    Maintaining Involvement 48

Regaining Attention 49
Ensuring Active Participation 49
Tight Parameters to Ensure Success 51
Do's and Don'ts 52

6. Enthrall 'Em All **54**
Job 1: Make Time Disappear 54
Infusing Excitement Into Sessions 54
Variety as a Vehicle 55
Monitoring an Audience 55
The 1–2–3 Rule 57
Questions and Answers 57
    Introductions Set the Tone 57
    Change of State 58
    Movement: More Than a Sign of Life,
       the Glue for Learning 59
    Energizers 60
    Breaks 62
    Putting Lecture in Its Place 62
    Covering Volumes of Content: Alternative Methods 63
    Accountability in Group Work 66
    Group Size 67
    Visuals to Enhance Meaning 67
    Directing Attention 69
    Applying Content 69
    Handling Questions 69
Do's and Don'ts 70

**7. Rave Reviews: Making Sure You Still
Have an Audience Left After Break** **72**
Appeal 72
Fun 72
Comfort 73
Mystery 73
Finesse 74
Questions and Answers 75
    When You Don't Have the Answer 75
    Building Fun Into Learning 75
    Creating Physical and Emotional Comfort 78
    Prizes and Rewards 80
    Meaningful Mixers 80

	Time and Organization	82
	Handling Difficult Audiences	83
	Humility	85
	Setting Yourself Apart	86
	Do's and Don'ts	88
8.	**That's a Wrap!**	**89**
	The Lasting Impression	89
	Questions and Answers	90
	The Three Features of a Quality Closer	90
	Audience Awareness of Session Gains	91
	Review, Rehearsal, and Application	92
	Positive Endings	97
	Do's and Don'ts	101
9.	**Evaluations: Make It the Best Plant Possible and Then Keep Weeding, Watering, and Talking to It Sweet**	**102**
	Consistency: An Allusive Target	102
	Inviting Improvement	103
	Questions and Answers	104
	Informal Feedback	104
	Formal Feedback	105
	Collegial Feedback	108
	Do's and Don'ts	110
	References	**111**
	Index	**113**

Preface

Sometimes change means doing things different.

Yogi Berra

Anyone standing before an audience, whether to facilitate, train, or entertain, is an agent of change. One session invites new ideas, another alters attitudes; some promote products, whereas others impart new skills. Yet in all cases, the desired result is to get the audience to *change*. And change is tough to get.

What the presenter thinks is exciting, sensible, and worthwhile might be perceived by others as unnecessary, incorrect, or confrontational. Even an entertaining speech can foster resistance! Want audience buy-in for your philosophy? Want their willingness to spend energy to learn a new skill? Hope for an unbridled enthusiasm for your content? It takes finesse and artistry. I laugh when clients who hire me preface their request with, "My veteran staff is somewhat resistant to change." An unknown sage once said, "Changing an institution is like moving a cemetery." Well, hang on. We have some movin' to do.

Yep, better bring in a lot of equipment.

ACKNOWLEDGMENTS

Corwin Press and the author extend their thanks to the following reviewers for their contributions to this volume: Marilee Sprenger, professional development consultant, presenter, and author; and Lynell Burmark, Thornburg Center associate, presenter, and author.

—Susan J. Jones

About the Author

 Susan Jones is a lifelong educator whose interest in best practice and research in teaching and learning led to a passion for effective communication. Although still facilitating and training education professionals, she currently devotes much energy to keynote speaking, training trainers of adult audiences in presentation skills, and facilitating institutional change. She has presented to more than 20,000 people in the past decade alone.

A leading expert on research-based classroom instruction and student achievement, she is the author of *Blueprint for Student Success: A Guide to Research-Based Teaching Practices, K-12* (2003), as well as articles and columns dealing with strategies to improve achievement. She is also a contributing author to two brain-research-based books. She can be contacted at sjjones@aug.com.

Introduction

Practice doesn't make perfect, nor is it supposed to. Practice is about increasing your repertoire of ways to recover from your mistakes.

Joann C. Gutin (Reader's Digest, January 2000)

Somewhere long ago (and before I was older than dirt), someone told me that people never really know how others perceive them. "Who you are" depends upon the observer's point of view. We see ourselves in one way; others see us in another—yet the two perspectives may have little to do with reality. For presenters, educators, and trainers of adult audiences, concern about how others perceive us is more than vain curiosity. Positive perception is essential to success.

From the get-go, a presenter's hands are full. It matters little whether the goal is to bring a change in ideas, attitude, or performance; *it is change*—and people, by their very nature, are resistant to it. One of the toughest lessons for the novice is that knowing your "stuff" doesn't guarantee you'll be well received, even when the "stuff" is good. Success requires planning, savvy performance, and sound communication. Presenting, you see, is an acquired skill, and a talent quite different from possessing wisdom. As such, it can be developed, refined, and perfected. In fact it must be—a lot of really smart people have been booed off stages.

Presenters and trainers can't rely on applause meters or audience comments to perfect skill. We need to know *why* a session fell flat today (no, it wasn't because of the brown suit), whereas yesterday the same training received a standing ovation. We need tried and true, nitty-gritty techniques that are indicators of excellence, tips of the stage, and rules of the platform. Only then can we ratchet presentations toward excellence.

I never planned on being a full-time presenter. After two decades in the classroom, a new position lured me to the world of adults where a part of my new job involved training. "No problem," I thought. I'd been delivering ideas and speaking before groups for years. *Whooooa, Rudy!* Working with audiences of peers was a whole new gig, and I had a *lot* to learn. But where was the rule book?

Determined that disaster was not going to deter me, I dragged myself to every presentation I could—not for the content, but to observe others practicing their skills in training. I generalized rules while I watched and then tried techniques that I spotted . . . and learned by trial and error. Observation, plus a couple of polishing courses and sage advice from veterans, gave me the confidence to risk flying by the seat of my pants. Inching toward excellence, my audience reviews reflected gradual progress. At first it was painful (many times!) and occasionally (enough to keep me going), truly exhilarating.

Years and years later (I didn't say I was a quick study), a clear picture has emerged regarding the difference between mediocrity and excellence in training adults. Oh, I'm still learning and I still experience occasional pain in the process. But audience reviews have become routinely positive, and I have spent increasingly less time getting tomato stains out of my work clothes. It seems only fair now to share what experience has taught me.

Backstage Pass is meant to put real teeth into the effectiveness of adult presenting. It is a rule book for rookies and veterans alike, with tips to speed the trainer's learning curve and eliminate the agony of trial and error, to avoid mistakes and leap—rather than inch—toward success. A word of caution (my grandmother taught me this one): really great ones don't avoid mistakes, they avoid *repeating* mistakes. It's hoped that each tip from *Backstage*, each correction, brings one ever closer to solid, consistent performance. It's not about us. It's about the impact we have on the audience in effecting change.

Come on backstage and watch how it's done.

CHAPTER ONE

Preparation Precedes Success

Before you run a marathon, you have to find your shoes.

Susan Jones

Luck is a matter of preparation meeting opportunity.

Oprah Winfrey

Good presenting looks easy. Audiences walk into organized rooms, tasks flow smoothly, and activities fit time slots perfectly. It is amazing how much effort goes into making it look effortless.

CLEAR COMMUNICATION: EXCEEDING EXPECTATIONS

Any presentation begins long before it starts: really, with the initial client contact. Clients who invite your services ask predictable questions: What are your fees? Availability? But before you agree to perform any service, *you* must ask questions—smart questions. What is the purpose of the session? The motive or goal of the client enlisting your services? What should attendees gain? Who will make up the

3

audience? Are facilities conducive to the session purpose? It's all crucial information:

- To ascertain that you are capable and willing to meet the needs of the audience and client
- To tailor your program to those needs.

If you're uncertain about exact expectations for a session, ask *more* questions and then clearly define what you would do to meet the goal. If it isn't enough to serve the client's purposes, bow out rather than disappoint. I always love the requests to work with staff to bring systemic change to the workplace and then be allotted a 2-hour session in which to do it. Nope, I don't think so. Honesty is the only way to go.

If you can do it, are willing to do it, and say you'll do it—the work of this first contact is still not complete. Make, as well, a verbal contract clearly stating what you'll provide—promising only that which you're certain you can deliver, at the highest quality with value added (a little more than expected—a bonus). A good rule of thumb is that for each day of presenting, there are two days of preparation and follow-up. Some of it is planning, some of it is handout preparation, and some is follow-up and reporting. Above all, don't promise what you *can't* provide—because the inevitable poor evaluations will later haunt you.

QUESTIONS AND ANSWERS

Minimizing the Chance for Misunderstanding

Q: How do I ensure that clients fully understand what to expect from me, since busy people forget phone conversations and the detail of verbal contracts?

A: Create an event file for each presentation. Routinely follow up conversations and verbal contracts with two communications to your contact: (1) A mailed or e-mailed hard copy contract that summarizes the service to be provided, event date and time, site, equipment needs, room set-up requests, and agreed arrangement for handouts and material supplies. Spell out your fees, expenses, and a payment timeline. (2) An e-mail summary of your understanding of session expectations, along with special requests or guidelines given to you. Print a reference copy of all communications for your event file. When preparing the presentation, reference and honor notes and requests—and if there's confusion, call or e-mail to clarify expectations.

Q. My clients are often busy people who expect me to remember every detail of conversations, but are hard to reach when I need them. Any suggestions?

A: Request names, numbers, and addresses of clients and any assistant involved in the project, so you can contact them and call them by name. It's often easier to reach secretaries for answers than the hiring client—and most assistants can handle issues or gain access to the person who can. Take notes on each conversation, date the note, and place it in the event file. Keep the file within arm's reach for speedy reference during follow-up calls about the upcoming job. Folks like to think they are your only audience and enjoy the personal touch when you reference a request, a comment, or an earlier action. Follow up with a brief e-mail summary of each conversation with the assistant, copying the hiring client.

Q: I have several projects going at a time. If someone calls, I don't think fast enough to be on top of a project. How can I avoid fumbling?

A: Keep all current project files boldly labeled and within arms reach, with dated conversation notes clipped to the inside cover. Your script is then at your fingertips. If you're unable to locate files and are not 100% certain of an answer, don't fumble. Ask to call back within minutes ("I have a client in my office" or "I'm on the other line") and do so, with information in hand.

Q: I am really conscientious about filling presentation requests. How do I avoid disappointment by failing to deliver what was envisioned for a session?

A: Never rely solely on memory to discuss or prepare presentations. You may think you know what the client wants ("I've done this dozens of times before"), but as added insurance 2–3 days prior to a presentation, check to be sure session needs have not changed. Also, a check midpoint during a presentation can ensure that you are delivering what is needed. The latter allows you to tweak as you go and really impresses a client!

Tailoring Programs: One Size Does Not Fit All

Q: Why do I need to tailor a program to an audience? My program is standardized.

A: Canned, prepackaged programs sooner or later lose their freshness, and audiences feel like something has been done *to* them, rather than *with* them. No two audiences are alike, and no single audience is the same twice. Even if you have an established program with defined content, *some* tailoring is in order—because *this* audience is more enthusiastic than the norm or more resistant. Each workplace climate uniquely impacts the receptivity of the content, and the level of sophistication differs from groups you've encountered before. Personal tailoring, even through embedded comments such as, "I know you are in the midst of budget cuts" or "with a 17% retention rate at Main Street School" establishes a connection. Any personal tailoring increases the likelihood of receptivity toward the presenter—on an emotional as well as intellectual level. Know your audience. Don't tap dance to entertain teenagers.

Preparing Handouts

Q: What about handouts—do I need them, and do they really matter?

A: Unless you are doing a short keynote address with the purpose of motivating or entertaining, you should have handouts. In all cases, form should follow function. Using PowerPoint or overhead transparencies with content? Audiences love thumbnails of the slides and space for note taking. It makes personal revisitation of information much easier and is especially appreciated by linear thinkers. In any case, order handouts to match the sequence of your presentation topics. Place any related articles, additional resources, or references at the end of the handouts (books, Web sites, articles). Don't forget to include your own contact numbers. This becomes value added and is appreciated by audiences.

Q: I get negative comments about my handouts. I include so much information! What more can I do?

A: "Stuff" is not enough. Again, be sure handouts mirror topic content, properly sequenced, so they don't appear disorganized or random. It's not enough for your presentation to hit the standard of excellence:

so too must your handouts. Just as mustard on your shirt, uncombed hair, and runs in hosiery raise eyebrows about your professionalism, so do below-par handouts. Sure to draw complaints are

Handouts that are handwritten (even if they are neat)

Poor quality copies of others' work

Text with spelling or punctuation errors

Use of trite, childish drawings (unless they are actually children's work)

No excuses for sloppiness or shlock work! Spell check is great, but doesn't replace good old-fashioned editing. In this age, anyone can produce professional quality handouts, *and should*. If you are unable to do it, find someone who can (or better yet, can teach *you* how!)

Q: Should handouts include full summaries of all material shared in the presentation or contain only skeletal outlines?

A: Take it off your plate. Make *participants* take notes—it helps them plant memory more efficiently, and it personalizes information. Individuals are more engaged when filling in note space under topic headings, discovering the three bulleted points, or filling in the blanks. They are more apt to *listen* for "the two reasons" if they're not already printed in front of them. Note-taking involves learners in content, as they go beyond listening to summarize and record ideas. Hint: Pause to allow folks to check their neighbor's notes for accuracy, as it's a great way to inspire small group discussion that doubles as a rehearsal. And skillful questioning inspires consideration of professional applications!

Q: Might it just be better to provide topic headings on otherwise blank sheets for note taking?

A: Participants enjoy receiving background articles or related topic resources, and they *want* copies of important information. When it is too voluminous or cumbersome for them to record themselves, provide it to them, either as an on-the-spot handout or by request via mail, e-mail, or phone. Anything I have to give legally and professionally is theirs (value added).

Organizing for Relaxed Delivery

Q: Even though I organize all pertinent information and sequence and write the presentation word for word as I want to deliver it, I'm still not relaxed. Nothing flows. What am I doing wrong?

A: Don't try to memorize a presentation word for word—to do so causes you to focus on recall of rigid, rote memory rather than the logical flow of concepts. Make communication of ideas the driving force during delivery rather than the replication of a memorized unit.

Plan and practice your presentation conceptually and logically. Identify the theme (what is my message?) and goal of the session (what do I want participants to leave with?). Then, identify and master key points, sequenced to transport the audience from the starting block to the finish line. Determine all explanations, tasks, and rehearsals necessary to ensure audience understanding of the key points, and then visualize the performance and rehearse until you have the sequence down pat. Be sure the mental outline flows logically toward the session goal. If you use written notes, work mainly off the sequenced key points—so as activities unfold and fundamentals are shared, the delivery is conversational and natural, not scripted.

Q: Aren't presenters and trainers really just performers?

A: Performing and presenting are fundamentally different. A performer is the focal point—a stand-alone entity, a spectacle to be observed. A presenter functions by connecting and interacting, either mentally or physically, with the audience. The presenter communicates with—not for—the audience.

DO'S AND DON'TS

- **Do** tailor every presentation to fit the audience and its unique needs
- **Do** promise only what you can deliver
- **Do** spend time on handouts—they matter!
- **Do** include handouts that reflect the content and sequence of the session
- **Do** provide copies of important overheads or slides
- **Do** make folks write, providing space for note taking
- **Don't** deliver a session from a script: connect, don't perform

CHAPTER TWO

Little Things Mean a Lot

If I had six hours to chop down a tree, I'd spend the first four sharpening the axe.

Abraham Lincoln, 1809–1865

Having the session planned, your mind focused, and handouts run off in sufficient numbers might seem enough. But before the curtain goes up, there's more to do! Some of it's ongoing, some relatively last minute—but each piece is integral to the whole.

SLEEP FOR EFFICIENCY

Most folks, given the chance, mentally run through and rehearse a presentation one last time immediately before delivering it. Sifting through scenarios and potential challenges helps one prepare, thereby increasing self-confidence and the likelihood of success. The problem is, who has *that* luxury? Too little time and presession commitments (like being stuck in traffic) interfere. Most morning sessions start too early to leisurely rehearse, so what do we do? Get up before the birds, load up on coffee, and go over our plans.

Presenters are like human candles, burning themselves at both ends—thinking they can do it all. We often neglect ourselves and ignore our most fundamental needs—like sleep. Adults require 8¼ hours of sleep per day according to University of Chicago sleep researcher Eve Van Cautier (Brink, 2000). Yes, Virginia, there is a need for sleep, and *adequate rest is more beneficial than sleeping less and rising early* to cram or organize. The National Sleep Foundation tells us tired brains don't function as efficiently as rested ones. Too little sleep can contribute to depression (good grief, we want you in a *positive* mood), as well as attention problems. Now I don't know about you, but when I have attention problems, I can't pay attention. Which leads directly to focus and flow glitches when I am presenting.

EAT FOR SUSTAINED ENERGY

Eating properly is also important. I know I am beginning to sound like your mother, but *you need breakfast* on the days you present! Not that bagel and diet pop as you run out the door, but a full breakfast of protein, fat, starch, and sugar. Starch and sugar alone (are we talking donut?) only sustain for about 1–2 hours. After that, blood sugar drops—with a subsequent decline in energy and the onset of hunger. Protein and fat included in the morning meal help slow the process of breaking down sugars, sustaining energy for longer periods of time.

Well, when my energy goes, I hit a wall. It's pretty tough to remain effective clutching the door molding to hold myself upright. When I feel better, I just plain do better. You will, too (Carper, 2000; Wolfe et al., 2000). According to Carper (2000) and Wolfe, Burkman, and Streng (2000), breakfast

- Reduces symptoms such as stomach pain, fatigue, and headache
- Allows for improved attention while performing tasks in late morning
- Improves the ability to retrieve information quicker and more accurately

- Reduces the likelihood of errors in problem solving
- Improves concentration performance in more complex tasks

Eggs, ham, toast, and jelly anyone?

Dress for Success

There are two basic rules for dressing, and neither has to do with runways or catalogs.

> **Rule 1:** Dress at least as well as the best dressed person in your audience. Leave the sequined dress in the closet if you are addressing teachers on an institute day, but put on your best suit if you are working with branch managers.

> **Rule 2:** Dress comfortably. Nothing ruins your presentation quicker than personal discomfort; the luxury of focusing on your audience evaporates if all you can think about is aching bunions or a protruding belly! So wear flat shoes if you need them. Put on loose pants or a waist-less dress so you don't have to hold your stomach in. No audience cares if you are high fashion (unless it's made up of adolescent girls, in which case after delivering a profound lecture, a hand will go up and someone will ask, "Where did you get your nail polish?").

Although you don't have to be mod to be appropriate, you *should* worry about lint on your lapel, runs in your hose, lipstick on your teeth, and pants that are too short. Audiences *do* notice that and figure that if you are slovenly in your appearance, you are sloppy in your thinking as well. They don't want tacky; they want classy. Women, in addition, must be careful to avoid anything alluring, as audiences can be offended. And if you are addressing a large audience, be sure you have either a pocket or belt to hold the lapel microphone box. Think classy. Think practical. Think comfortable.

Pack Light and Catch the Early Train

There was a time that I took resource books to share, plus every prop and tool that could possibly be used for a session (just in case). By the time I lugged the bulk and weight and set up the room, I was thoroughly exhausted. Besides, trying to repack quickly to catch a flight or beat traffic was a stressor I didn't need. Supplies ended up thrown in bags, so reorganizing for the next day was a *big* chore.

Learn from my mistakes. Take only what is absolutely essential, plus one thing more. Carry a filler activity to bail out of a tough spot (maybe props for an energizer or a transparency with a brain teaser), something that can be used and adapted to any audience, anywhere if there is a late start or an unexpected lull. Pack essential business and personal items in a roller bag (tape, extra transparencies, etc.) and restock after each session. Plan for disaster and hope for smooth waters (what's that adage? Murphy's Law—anything that can go wrong, sooner or later does).

QUESTIONS AND ANSWERS

Packing Checklist

Q: So exactly what are your secrets in terms of items to pack?

A: Well, having arrived 3 minutes prior to a session's start with road dirt up to my elbows from changing a flat tire, I've learned to bring travel wet cloths. They don't remove grease, but do help in the general dirt category. Having been stranded in airports overnight but expected nonetheless to present at the crack of dawn without time to clean up in a hotel (never mind sleep), I always have a toothbrush and small container of toothpaste tucked in my traveling bag. Did you know there are deodorant wipes? Pack a couple—it's peace of mind. Not to mention participants appreciate them. Women wearing hosiery should tuck a backup pair in their presentation bag, and everyone should carry a lint brush.

Q: You talk about personal items—any professional supplies you recommend taking, beyond the computer or overheads?

A: Are there ever. I always bring masking tape, but never on a roll—too bulky. Instead, wrap strips of tape around the shaft of Vis-à-Vis pens, ready to peel off when needed. To provide tape for use by others, cut squares of waxed paper and stick strips of masking tape to it—these can be divided into smaller squares and distributed to tables for group use in mounting chart paper, etc. Bring along a small travel clock or watch with numbers large enough to see at a glance (so you don't need to hold it within 2 inches of your face) as many rooms lack clocks. Have an electric plug adapter in case you need another outlet. Take an ample supply of write-on transparencies *in* their cardboard box. Remove about one third of them to provide a little storage space (this leaves plenty for a full day's training). Tuck a few critical items in the space:

- A pocket tissue packet on top of the clean transparencies
- Vis-à-Vis pens, with duplicates of the most used (for me, that's black and blue)
- Everything needed for an overhead or projection device (pen, pointer, scissors, computer cables, and adapters)

When the session is over, all pens, remaining tissues, and so forth go back in and are rubber banded shut for storage in the presentation bag. The box is closed with three heavy rubber bands (so if one breaks, there are backups) to avoid a spill in your suitcase. No dumping, no spilling, no bulk.

Q: I fly to presentations. How do I bring scissors?

A: I always store scissors in my transparency box for local work; for jobs that require commercial flying, scissors are a permanent fixture in my check-on bag. Make them the blunt-nose, plastic children's variety so that if you forget to take them out of your carry-on presentation bag, you won't be thrown in the pokey for carrying contraband.

Q: Why do you take a pointer? Isn't that why I have a finger?

A: Don't use your finger! It's distracting for the audience to see that chubby digit projected over the top of your wonderful visual. Special pointers can be purchased, but swizzle sticks work as well. Me? I use the pointed end of a fountain pen, which is always at hand—in my transparency box. A laser pointer is best when using a computer-based program.

Sharing Book Resources

Q: Because of the topics on which I present, I share books that are timely and valuable to enhance my presentation. Folks want to see the books which I recommend, but I am just plain bogged down trying to bring them all with me.

A: Don't bring them! Nine out of ten times, only a handful of people actually thumb through the books. What they want is to see what the book *looks* like: plus the title and author of those most interesting. They will seek them out for closer scrutiny on their own time. Instead of hauling along 4 tons of publications, scan and create transparencies or slides of book covers you want to share. No bulk to carry, it's easier for the audience to see from their seats anyway, and if folks want to read the table of contents, make a slide of it (or a reusable, laminated copy mounted on a wall or table) for folks to view during break time.

Heading Off Equipment Trouble

Q: I have arrived at a session to discover no—or a poorly functioning—projection device. How do you handle that gracefully?

A: Purchasing and carrying your own projection device is about the only way to avoid poor quality equipment. Of course, it means you will be adding back that bulk from the books you left behind in the office! If the expense or trouble of bringing your own device is prohibitive, then at least be certain that you bring backup cables and extension cords. Back up the presentation on a CD that could run on a computer they provide, should yours fail to interface with their equipment. Most important, if you use a PowerPoint presentation, carry every slide in transparency form, properly sequenced in a secure folder. Routinely request an overhead projector and screen in addition to a projection device when arranging for equipment with a client. That way, you can record items and leave them projected while PowerPoint is presenting, using both tools simultaneously. It allows spontaneity that would be missing with a fully mechanical display!

Q: How do I avoid distracting my audience with the constant glare of an overhead?

A: Constant illumination is a visual distraction but turning a projector on and off burns out expensive bulbs. To solve the problem, leave the overhead motor and bulb continuously on, but cover the projector surface when not in use. I encase my presenter notes in a tag board file folder, which doubles as an overhead surface cover when opened. For the same reason, hit the "b" key to go to black screen after each regular slide in a PowerPoint presentation to eliminate visual distraction between slides. Simply hit it again and you return to the slide you left.

Q: Why take transparencies? I use PowerPoint.

A: For two reasons. First, if you have last-minute ideas or a request for information that is not on a formal presentation slide, you can handle it using an overhead. And second, if your PowerPoint system has a glitch, you can use your backup transparencies to bail you out. I have been saved more than once by backup transparencies. Another reason why you need to have the overhead projector handy!

Hydration—Wet Your Whistle to Whet Your Brain

Q: My throat gets dry when I present. Is it all right to set a cup of coffee or a soft drink on the table when I present?

A: When you are thirsty, drink—but limit your choice to water. A rule of thumb is to drink 1 quart of water daily per 100 pounds of body weight. When a person is stressed (and presenting can be stressful!), as much as three times as much water is needed. A hydrated brain increases the likelihood of higher performance (Fahey, 2000).

Q: Why water? I prefer soft drinks, coffee, or iced tea.

A: You need fluids that hydrate, not dehydrate, your brain. Diuretics, including coffee, tea, carbonated beverages, and chocolate (alcohol, too) drive up the salt level in the body by eliminating water, thus upsetting the balance of water in and outside of brain cells. Overuse of diuretics may actually decrease brain potential. Water, in addition to aiding digestion, enables the brain to focus attention and process faster during higher-level thinking and is essential for electrical transmissions in the brain needed for sensing, thinking, and learning.

Do's and Don'ts

- **Do** eat breakfast on presentation days
- **Do** dress comfortably
- **Do** plan ahead to eliminate glare when using visual media
- **Do** anticipate trouble
- **Do** bring backup transparencies for a slide presentation
- **Do** keep your brain hydrated
- **Don't** dress more casually than your audience
- **Don't** use a finger as a pointer for transparencies

CHAPTER THREE

Lights, Camera, Action!

The main thing is to keep the main thing the main thing.

Stephen Covey

READYING THE FACILITY

You've arrived! And chances are the room is too dark, too large, or too small—but no matter. Deal with it. Start with an assessment of the facility. Is the presenter's table situated a workable distance from the audience? Do audience chairs need to be moved or tables arranged?

Since dark rooms put people to sleep, make the room as bright as possible without creating screen glare. Test and focus the overhead, hook up, and check that projection devices are functioning properly. If the available screen is too low, too scratched, or too small for the audience to see, remove it and substitute a blank, light colored wall to project upon. Then, turn attention to the details.

Figure 3.1

Room Setups . . .

*can encourage or stifle participation. Choose a setup
that serves your presentation purpose best.*

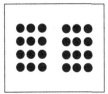

Theater-style seating is the least conducive to interaction and participation by attendees, but gives the instructor full control of the session. Short keynotes or informational sessions are appropriate for such a room arrangement.

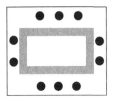

The **rectangular** shaped setup allows moderate control by the presenter/facilitator, as well as moderately good views for charts and visuals. The participation level likely is only moderate.

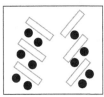

The **herringbone** setup allows moderate control by the presenter/facilitator and encourages high levels of participation by an audience. Participants are easily able to see each other, the instructor, and visuals.

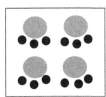

Half rounds allow for moderate instructor control, and high levels of participation are possible. High visibility is likely for the instructor, for participants to view visuals, and between participants.

U-shaped setups allow high levels of instructor control, but provide only moderate visibility of the facilitator and visuals for the audience. This setup also limits participation and interaction by the audience.

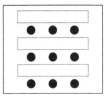

Classroom-style setups discourage participation by the audience, but increase to high levels the control possible by the instructor. Visibility of charts, screens, and the instructor is low.

Materials

Unless you are making a keynote speech from a podium, you'll likely need a presentation table from which to work. My preference is one large enough to accommodate projection equipment, a disc player, and all incidental materials. Unpack and arrange supplies in a way that works for you, even if it means repositioning the table or replacing it with a makeshift surface. Set up your computer, or if you are using transparencies, place them, properly sequenced, next to the overhead. Leave a space above or to the side to stack them after use, in order. Open your write-on transparency box, and flip all the "stuff" (except the blank transparencies) into the lid: tissue, pens, Vis-à-Vis pens, and scissors. Use this as their resting place during the presentation, where they remain, ready for use. That way, pens don't roll onto the floor, you're not in search of elusive scissors, and materials are at your fingertips. Place the box where it can be easily reached and near the box half that contains blank transparencies. Hook up your music (I love to set up while music plays), and if you are not relying on a computer or iPod to produce it, lay out any CDs that you anticipate using. This saves fumbling later, and is made even better if you lay a key card out referencing exact tracks you want to use for each CD. Zap the disc in, advance quickly to the track you want, and hit pause—then all you need is to hit "play" when it is time for music. I have found the simplest way to amplify music is to lay a lavalier microphone next to the CD speaker and pump it through the room's sound system. Finally, distribute or arrange materials and handouts. You're ready to go!

Start Before You Begin

When possible, stop all preparations 15 minutes before the session begins to greet arriving participants. Brief personal conversations win audience approval and can be a most valuable part of the day. The likelihood of audience cooperation during the training increases, and positive, relaxed interaction provides *you* with insights about *their* expectations and helps you meet the needs peculiar to a group. It's surprising how many folks comment on a presenter who actually *visits* with them!

And there's a bonus; speaking casually with audience members helps any presenter relax. Fifteen minutes of visiting eliminates lead-up time often fraught with stress and anxiety. Better to be laughing and learning than wringing hands and reading through your notes.

QUESTIONS AND ANSWERS

Crutches to Stay Calm and on Course

Q: What do I do if I practice and practice, even memorizing my presentation, but lose my train of thought when my session begins?

A: Don't memorize your presentation. Remember, a script often equates to a stiff delivery (see Chapter 1). Worse yet, it can cause panic at getting lost. Instead, practice and visualize your presentation prior to its delivery, mastering key points and the session's activity sequence. Then if your mind wanders, reference notes listing key points to steer you back on course and delivery will appear spontaneous.

Q: It's not the key points, it's the details that elude me when I am stressed.

A: Use crutches to put you at ease and on track. If using PowerPoint, carefully create slides that accurately reflect the presentation sequence and include key words to guide your train of thought. If you use overhead transparencies, invest in transparency covers: clear encasements that envelop the transparency itself, edged in light cardboard flaps. On those flaps write notes referencing details of the key points so it appears you are speaking from memory, while you are actually reading notes no one else can see!

Q: What if I am recording ideas on a chart pad? Should I work off note cards so I don't forget details and look foolish?

A: Copying information, whether off a notepad or note cards, makes a presenter look inept (unless attempting to quote a passage exactly, in which case it's fine). What you want to do is minimize the chances for forgetting, so you appear capable and in command of content. Before participants arrive, use a light lead pencil to sketch or record important details on charts you'll use during the session. Participants will NOT be able to see your sketches (even the front row folks), and you will feel confident by simply overwriting prewritten light notes with heavy marker and letting your charts unfold during the seminar.

Room Setup: The Good, the Bad, and the Adjustments

Q: Does room setup really matter?

A: You bet. Although choices are not always available, if you do have your druthers, avoid theater-style seating unless the session is a lecture and of very short duration (preferably an hour or less). For sessions in which the purpose is to create a product, tangible or intangible, participants require tables that seat folks in space and numbers that enable all to see and touch the work area. If the training includes lecture and small group interaction, semicircle or half-round tables work best, with participants facing the facilitator.

Q: What if I have no choice—the group is large, the seminar is long, and the only available space is an auditorium. Am I doomed to failure?

A: Of course not! The session does demand creative planning and skilled presenting, however. I've conducted whole-day sessions with great success in auditoriums, but only by including continual opportunities for movement and interaction between participants. Build in quick, interactive tasks that participants accomplish by turning around or side-to-side and giving the audience frequent, short breaks to make the confinement bearable. When possible, include a few highly interactive tasks that move participants physically to another portion of the auditorium. Note that for tasks requiring physical relocation, the auditorium's capacity must be substantially larger than the audience size to allow comfortable movement and adequate workspace. Don't forget to build extra time into the session agenda for this—movement and interactive tasks take time.

Seating Participants for Great Results

Q: At times, I present in a very large room to a very small group of people. People tend to scatter when they sit, and when I ask them to cluster or move toward the front of the room, they refuse. How can I do this without getting everyone testy?

A: You're wise to be concerned. Once you've raised their ire, you've lost them—so you must nip trouble in the bud. Anticipation coupled with a little advance work really pays. Arrive at the seminar site well before the start of a session. Provide only enough chairs and tables for the anticipated number of folks, minus a few—remove any excess. This forces participants to fill all seats in the room. However, don't leave extra tables in the back of the room; participants are smart cookies and will move chairs to them to avoid sitting up front. Remove tables altogether or place them so far from the seminar area that they are unusable. If there is an overflow crowd, *add* more chairs around the existing tables even if there is slight crowding. (Just don't get it so crowded that folks have no room for coffee cups, note pads, and materials. Then you have a room full of grumps and are right back where you started.) An extra one or two people at a table are fine: beyond that, set up another table to accommodate. Group energy is better than group scatter; reaction and interaction really suffer when folks are too spread out.

Q: What if I can't move tables or remove chairs?

A: Make it inconvenient for them to be seated anywhere except where you want them. In an auditorium, it is fair game to block off rows by taping off access to them, leaving only those toward the front or center open. Tilt chairs against tables to indicate their unavailability and greet people as they enter, requesting they avoid tilted chairs. Couple this with the placement of handouts or activity materials only at tables where you want folks to sit, and the message is loud and clear as to the appropriate seating areas. At session start, express your appreciation for folks sitting only where materials are placed. Give a general explanation why by focusing not on their needs, but on your needs (i.e., "I can't project my voice to the back of the room," "I'll need to monitor activities," or "Special seating is necessary for our planned activities"). Yada, yada, yada.

Q: If the room is too large for the audience, does it really matter if participants are spread thinly throughout the room?

A: It sure does! People need to be comfortably clustered to achieve group energy. Adults feed off each other for excitement, engagement, and interaction. Your ideas will be better received, your jokes will get bigger laughs, and audience enthusiasm will skyrocket when people are seated closely. If you are expecting thirty people but only ten come, invite participants to move chairs in a circle or cluster with you in a corner of the room. Nothing makes a high-quality presentation fall flat faster than an audience too spread out to bond in response.

Q: The closer the better, right?

A: Wrong. Comfortably close is the key. Overly crowded personal space is a stressor that negatively influences creativity and cognition. The rule of thumb is that individuals need adequate space to perform activities, which can mean room for notebooks, computers, paper, elbows, and water glasses.

Distributing Handouts and Materials

Q: You mention materials and supplies—how in the world can I place all handouts and materials at tables or chairs before the audience arrives, make it look neat and organized, finish early enough to devote 15 minutes before the session to greet people, and not be exhausted before the session begins?

A: Disseminate all essential materials prior to the opening of very short sessions. However, *if there's adequate time* within the session, handouts can be dispersed at the time they're referenced in the presentation. Not only does it reduce setup time, but passing out or picking up by participants requires physical movement, which provides a mental and physical break that keeps folks engaged. Also, training flexibility increases by withholding materials until they are needed, as it is easier to add or eliminate activities. If all materials are provided up front, when time runs short or you determine a task is unnecessary, participants might feel cheated when materials aren't used. You want your audience to believe they experienced a full, complete session and weren't shortchanged in any way—even if they were!

Charts, Slides, and Overheads

Q: I love using charts and colored markers, as it seems far more personal when working with a group. Is it OK to use them in place of slides or transparencies?

A: Yes, but . . . charts as a primary tool for either communicating or recording information are appropriate only for small group facilitations of fifteen to twenty people, tops. More than that and many audience members won't be able to see clearly enough to read what's recorded and will eventually stop trying. That doesn't mean that charts have no place in a large group presentation; it simply means that their function changes. Charts are effective when smaller subgroups work on tasks and need to record information. They are also useful for displaying small group products for large group viewing in a carousel process.[1]

Q: No matter how hard I try, when I use overheads they slip, turn, and project partly off the screen.

A: When you set up a projector, carefully position a transparency on the screen until it's straight and focused. Then, either draw a thin, erasable Vis-à-vis line or place a piece of masking tape on the screen against which to align all subsequent transparencies.

Q: I can't fit all the text on the screen. If the ceiling is high, I can. But I present in 8- and 10-foot-high rooms.

A: If you have difficulties fitting all text on the screen, you might have too much text! Use only key words—three lines, three to six words per line—and flesh information with your verbal explanation. Another important guideline is to place text and visuals on the top one half to one third of the slide or transparency so that everyone—even those toward the back of the room—can see it clearly when projected.

Grand Entrances

Q: When presenting a keynote address, do I just wait on stage until introduced? I want to make a positive first impression.

A: If you have a choice (and you don't always), enter in a brisk and self-assured way from either the back of the room or the left side of the stage. Either way, adjust the microphone position to your height or ensure that the lapel mike is securely anchored *before* you speak. Pause to let the audience drink you in visually and begin with a commanding, clear, and measured voice. Then let 'er rip.

Q: I am a keynote and public speaker. Should I greet and meet the audience 15 minutes before a speech or is that something that only benefits trainers?

A: Absolutely, do it. Now there are times when, logistically or practically speaking, it's impossible. But when possible, I mix and speak with audiences prior to keynote addresses. However, 3–5 minutes before start time, disappear and position yourself for the grand entrance.

Q: If session participants are running late, should I delay the start to accommodate? It's so clumsy to begin when a third of the folks haven't yet arrived!

A: Commence any session 4–5 minutes past the designated start time, but no more—even when there's a legitimate personal excuse (flat tire). People don't feel put upon with a short delay, but when longer, it rankles those who are prompt. Begin, and ignore individuals who straggle in. It'll be their problem to catch up and will send this message: *time is honored.* The same promptness should extend to resumption after breaks as well. Note: If an entire audience is delayed (snow storm), that's different. Delay your start with an OK from the hiring client. If a substantial number of participants have a common, legitimate excuse for arriving late (East Side Bridge is closed), announce that you are going ahead even though many people are delayed and request they help latecomers fill in notes, and so forth. You appear sensitive, but also cognizant of the need to use time wisely and efficiently.

Do's and Don'ts

- **Do** cluster folks for group energy
- **Do** place materials on tables you want used and not on those you want left vacant
- **Do** use charts for small group work to record and share information
- **Do** start on time
- **Don't** use charts as a primary communication piece with more than twenty people

Note

1. A carousel process enables individuals or groups to circulate simultaneously to view collegial products or materials—allowing ongoing reflection and conversation.

CHAPTER FOUR

Quick—Let 'em Love You!

More acceptable is the character of the straightforward man . . .

The Teaching for Merikare,
c. 2135–2040 BC (Bartlett, 1982)

GAINING ACCEPTANCE

So you think you have the whole thing licked, what with your extensive preparations and your 15-minute welcome. Au contraire! Somewhere years ago, I heard that a public speaker has 5 minutes to win over an audience. I'd wager it's a lot less than that.

Let's get one thing straight. The audience *wants* to like you! That's quite different, however, from them actually *doing* it. People often press me for a list of what really *makes* the difference between acceptance and hostility. Okay. Here's the short list:

1. Vulnerability

2. Establishing common ground

3. Friendly is good—familiar is not

4. Honoring knowledge and know-how

Building Audience Rapport

Vulnerability

Vulnerability means showing you're human and susceptible to criticism, attack, and hurt feelings (actually, it's true—presenters *are* thin skinned). Don't be an ice princess or a steel warrior—tell stories of your failures (and how you overcame them), show emotion and enthusiasm when talking, and admit mistakes you make (whether in spelling or judgment). When caught in error, admit it, perhaps saying something lighthearted or self-deprecating: "Another senior moment!" or "Don't you hate it when this happens?" or "Imagine my embarrassment!" Sincere, yet light.

One caution in the sharing feelings department: don't become overly emotional or sappy. I'll never forget the facilitator in a session I attended some years ago. He became so emotional in the midst of his delivery that he actually perched on a stool and wept—in front of the audience! He morphed from vulnerable to weak in just moments, at least in my mind. He lost his credibility, and he lost me. There's a line in professional communication between empathy and raw, personal emotion you don't want to cross.

Establish Common Ground

Identify commonalities with your audience up front in opening remarks. If the audience is composed of teachers, refer to teaching experiences that you have had. If working with a human resource staff, explain your interest or experience in that area. But don't read a vita to your listeners! Simply acknowledge that you understand their struggles and interests and share them. It's as simple as that.

Friendly Is Good, Familiar Is Not

Friendliness should never evolve into familiarity when it comes to presenting and facilitating. Finding common ground doesn't mean becoming overly familiar with participants. Speak personally but only on professional topics, and you'll remain in safe territory. When feelings are exposed or shortcomings shared outside the realm of professional topics, contact becomes social and is counterproductive. Presenters need to be vulnerable, not commonplace; all like to think that the expert or leader has special qualities that entitle them to respect. Errors? Always. Struggles? Indeed. Success in the end? Yes. Don't disappoint. And don't be a complainer.

Acknowledge Knowledge and Know-How

Acknowledge audience knowledge and know-how within the first few minutes of any session, honoring participant expertise and noting personal and collective experience. Rest assured, somebody in that audience already knows any piece of information you're about to present. Sending the message that you are expert above all others makes you a target that some audience participant is eager to bring down a notch or two.

WORKING AROUND PERSONAL QUIRKS

Presenters are not robots. In spite of the best intentions, each of us possesses personal shortcomings of which we are aware and on which we work but can't seem to totally eliminate. Mine? Which one? The worst is that I am LOUD. So much, in fact, that I still hold my high school's record (40+ years' worth) for "thespian least needing a mike" in an auditorium built for 5,000. But that's another story. The fact is that you can get the audience to overlook some of these behaviors by cutting criticism off at the pass. How? Hedge on your perceived shortcomings! Anticipate what will annoy or aggravate an audience and warn them up front about it. I usually tell the audience that I am loud—and know it. "Under no circumstances do I want to offend anyone, so please let me know if my booming voice is too much." I have never had a complaint about my loudness since doing this, but I sure had a few comments on evaluations prior to using the early warning system. Of course, I continuously work on correcting my shortcomings, as well.

QUESTIONS AND ANSWERS

Q: People may be willing to forgive too loud or soft a voice if warned up front. Anything else you can head off at the pass?

A: Oh, yes. Wise presenters include more than they anticipate needing, in both materials and information. Handouts often include materials for a host of activities never used during a presentation (sometimes planned that way, often for lack of time to finish). Rather than letting folks feel they didn't do everything and hence were shortchanged, tell them right up front that handouts contain information beyond that which you expect to cover—to give more depth and more resources for their personal interest and follow-up. If your problem is remembering to give breaks, ask the audience to remind you to provide them if you forget, or remind you to turn off a projection device, or refocus an overhead if you routinely forget to do it on your own—whatever you anticipate as a predictable oversight on your part! You must work to minimize the number of errors and then try to remedy them in subsequent trainings, but hedging a little helps avoid immediate criticism and allows folks to see you as vulnerable, but striving. People love that you're human, just like them.

Honoring Audience Expertise

Q: I understand why honoring expertise is important. But how is it done?

A: There are a variety of ways. With a very large group, simply ask for a show of hands. "How many in the audience have worked at XYZ for at least 2 years? 5 years? 10 years?" Then comment upon their impressive experience and that there is nothing you can say that someone in the room doesn't already know. With smaller groups, perhaps use an opening mixer that asks participants at each table to add up their total years of experience. Tables report out quickly while you tally the numbers, arriving (undoubtedly) at a huge total. "Do you realize, in this small group, we have over 732 years of experience?" If time and debrief logistics allow, use peer reporting of impressive service or accomplishments. Or inquire from your hiring client informational details about employee experience, and note them publicly. Be impressed, be humble when comparing your expertise with theirs collectively. As an old sage once said, be sincere whether you mean it or not (that's a joke, honest). The bottom line? You defuse defensiveness by acknowledging accomplishment. Participants no longer need to compete with you, but can learn *with* you. You serve as a conduit.

Q: I present often to veteran audiences. Should I list my accomplishments to establish credibility?

A: No. To do so makes it appear to many in the audience that you are *above* them. You lose your vulnerability and invite nitpicking to test your knowledge. Instead, mention briefly your background, almost in passing—but never in a way to flaunt the many experiences that you have. The appropriate place for a list of accomplishments is with a formal introduction, *given by someone else*. Once *you* begin to speak, lay off the list of accomplishments and talk to folks from experience, highlighting those pertinent to your audiences and relating to your message. Folks will be put off by comments about your flight in from Prague, the research project at Harvard, and tea with the queen. Sorta puts you above them, if you know what I mean.

Increasing Visibility

Q: Podium or not, when giving a keynote?

A: An amazing thing is folks not only want to hear your words, but they want to *see* you. Let them. A rule of thumb? Position yourself under a spotlight if there is one, so your face is lit and body movement can be scrutinized. Stand behind the podium as little as possible while still functioning comfortably so people can view the entire you (another reason why it's nice to wear loose clothing so folks can only speculate about your model-perfect body).

Changing an Audience's Point of View

Q: At times, I bump into an audience that wants to derail what I am trying to accomplish. How in the world do I get them to listen when their vision of truth is so conflicted with my message?

A: It is doable, with finesse. Let the audience identify the factors, the features, the foundational qualities important to *them*. Accept, record, and use them as criteria to reflect upon and connect with *your* purposes and points. If your idea or strategy is diametrically opposed to principles and methods practiced by your audience, start by asking participants what problems they struggle to overcome each day. List them and show how *your* techniques accomplish what they want. Improving workplace productivity? Ask what their personal experiences show most hinders or helps productivity. Find at least one point of agreement. Mention that common ground, honor it (establishing a common set of beliefs), and go forward.

Let me give a personal example. I often begin workshops for extremely traditional teachers by mentioning the importance of routine in the classroom. The approach never yet has failed me, as those audiences figure if I believe in routines, I know something! Find a quality or premise on which you and most audience members agree, and go from there. I'll never forget the day a gentleman, whom the hiring client identified as the most resistant employee on staff, came up to shake my hand at break, telling me, "You are the first so-called expert who's ever made sense. Thanks!" You see, we had a common foundation.

Honor feelings, discover commonalities, and validate that which is already correct. Use the common threads as vehicles for transitioning from where the audience is to where you hope to take them. It gains immediate buy-in. Folks don't argue with their own data, and they don't find fault with their own conclusions. Ah, audience rapport.

Q: Do personal stories and illustrations build rapport with an audience?

A: To garner and maintain rapport with the whole group, be open and generous with what you share. Use personal illustrations as examples of key points. Tell *your* story. Speak not only of your successes and discoveries, but of your struggles and frustrations. You, like them, have trials and tribulations, highs and lows, and successes and disappointments.

Agendas and Overviews

Q: Sometimes clients ask for agendas. Is providing them a good idea?

A: Agendas are fine—to list key points and their sequence in a presentation. My recommendation is to provide general categories of topics and the order of their discussion, but *never put times* on them! Why include only broad categories and not detailed subtopics? Because if you choose to omit any item listed, participants will question your motives. Why no specific times or time allotments? Because if you are ahead of schedule, participants count on being dismissed early. Not a good assumption. If you run over on the next topic, they'll be aggravated because now they're behind. And besides, if you allocate 30 minutes for a section of the training but it runs to 42, audience members can get agitated and cease to focus on the topic. Instead, they fret that they'll be expected to stay late to finish. Don't invite trouble. What audiences don't know doesn't hurt them.

Q: Are agendas a must?

A: No. I rarely use them. But I accomplish their purpose (providing the overview and scope for the training) in other ways—read on:

Q: I have been criticized for not being organized. I am! I know what I need to cover and do it efficiently. How do I make my plans and progress clear to the audience?

A: First, audiences should be told in the first few minutes why they are in your audience and what your expectations and purposes are for the day. Lay it out in broad and general terms. Avoid specificity, so if you need to omit a subsection, the audience will never know and thus never feel slighted. Use an opening visual to list key areas for the session, and then reference each as you transition through the training. Recap all areas at session end to drive home the organization and thoroughness of your presentation (logical, analytical folks love this).

Introductions and Openers

Q: Do I need a formal mixer or opener to break the ice?

A: As a rule of thumb, yes. It may be incorporated into intragroup introductions or done as a whole audience activity. Either way, ensure that it's fast and lighthearted, with a time reminder about halfway through to afford each individual ample opportunity to actively participate. Any mixer should relate in some way to an underlying principle or skill topic of the overall session. If you are team building, for example, incorporate interdependent activities into the mixer. Then reference the theme to segue into the training message.

Q: Are introductions between participants important?

A: In training sessions and presentations in which people are expected to interact or generate a product of any sort, yes. Introductions should reflect upon something that brings into focus the practicality of the training (Greatest challenge facing you? Greatest success? What would make this day worth your time and effort?).

Figure 4.1

Openers

A. For Willing Participants: Instead of simply asking participants to introduce them-selves to colleagues with descriptions of their work tasks, ask them to name the great-est gift they could hope to gain from the day's training and the greatest contribution *they* can make to the day's training. At the end of the session, related follow-up ques-tions might be asked: What did you *bring* – What have you *received*? Simple ques-tions such as these honor expertise and lay groundwork for self-esteem, value, buy-in, and reflection.

B. Negative Buster: When attendees resent time away from the office, or think they know it all and shouldn't be required to attend a training, dispel negative thoughts in a lighthearted and fast-paced activity. Post ten chart papers with one inflated balloon next to each. Open the session with an observation that you have heard some grumbling about attendance at this workshop and do a fast listing of the top ten reasons the topic or the session won't work for them (or why their valuable time should not be wasted attending it). Start the process yourself, with a comment like "It's boring because it involves obvious information that I already know," or "I'm too busy for this." Record each offered complaint on a single chart, moving quickly as you progress. After recording ten complaints, go back to #1 and dispel it. "You already know this? Super—we need your expertise and guidance, rooted in your deep experience." Then pop the balloon to sym-bolize the dispelling of the gripe. Or #2 — "You're right, you ARE too busy. But if we waited until the time was right for having kids, the human species would have died out eons ago!" POP. Continue until all negatives are dispelled and begin afresh with training.

Adapted from *Too Busy for Training?*
Creative Training Techniques, December, 1997.

C. Getting to Know You: A great way to get deeper, quick connections between people who know little about one another before they attend a session is to ask participants to form small groups of two to three people. After groups are formed, ask each person to take four different items from their wallet, purse, briefcases, or pockets that best represent the following and share them with group members:

- Something memorable
- Something revealing
- Something priceless
- Something worthless

Folks enjoy sharing their own choices, as well as learning about colleagues!

Q: I love the inclusion of energizers in long sessions I attend. Any guidelines for using them?

A: Audiences need changes of state (a mental shifting of gears to break monotony or end mental lethargy, allowing the brain to focus anew with full attention). Such changes can come from shifts in pace, energy level, or task type. I have two tips. If your audience has been sitting 45 minutes or more prior to your start, *begin* with an energizer before welcomes, introductions, and overviews! Ask the audience to move, or laugh, or stretch—something that changes their state and allows them to reengage mentally and physically to your presentation. That leads to the second tip. Energizers should be inserted *whenever* the audience has been sitting and participating in a monotonous way for 30 minutes without any change of state.

If people take a physical break (12+ minutes for restroom or snacks), or shift tasks to a reverse activity (i.e., from listening to reflecting, from reading to explaining, from whole group debrief to lecture), then there is no urgency for an energizer. An energizer is like a breather, providing a shift in concentration and activity to allow the brain and body to continue on. That shift can come through a change of activity or energizer-breathers.

Q: Even when I do great openers and energizers, folks connect with each other, but not me! Any ideas?

A: Make eye contact to connect. Looking someone in the eye communicates sincerity and credibility. Practice focusing on one person's face at a time while delivering training and watch your words register.

Positive Communication

Q: There must be something intangible that affects audience response. Sometimes I listen to presenters and just plain don't like them. How about that?

A: Energy might be that intangible something! Your eye, mouth, and facial muscles can improve rapport with others or destroy it. Avoid frowning, rolling eyes, or frequent grimacing. It may sound silly, but practice smiling and learn what a "pleasant" face feels like by looking in the mirror and then replicate that feeling when you present.

Next, put power behind your presentation. A tense body, poor posture, or poor breath control negatively influences voice timbre and tempo. Stretch and loosen up to release energy if you find yourself speaking too quickly. Breathe deeply before making key points; insert pauses and vary speaking tempo. Videotaping for self-assessment (or collegial review) can really help in this area. Listen to your recorded voice and determine its effectiveness; then watch your body and facial communication without sound to monitor nonverbals. Finally, reflect on your overall impact by combining sound and visuals. It can be an eye opener. Remember, it's about communication *effectiveness.*

Q: I love music, but am reluctant to use it in my presentations. A good idea, or not?

A: As long ago as May 1980, an editorial in the *Journal of the American Medical Association* stated, "Music activates the life energy and reduces one's vulnerability to stress." Music is a super tool! Use calming, pleasant music as participants enter the room initially and the same type of music as they exit for breaks and lunch. When they reenter to resume training, however, increase the tempo of your music to be faster and more upbeat to reenergize the audience and put them in the mood to tackle the subject again. I also find music a great backdrop for energizers and mixer tasks and a soothing background for quick-paced small group reviews. Because room activity drowns out the average CD player or computer, laying my lapel or hand mike on the speaker works well to amplify sound throughout the facility.

Q: Any music that's a guaranteed winner?

A: I find variety is the answer—that way, you hit upon something for everyone. I alternate between classical, Clapton, swing bands, Uncle Cracker, Dylan instrumentals, Louis Armstrong—anything that's upbeat and pleasant. Provide variations in tempo, but keep the music rather generic to avoid any genre that might offend, even if only a small portion of the audience. I have found that jazz, blues, and rap reap negative reviews from some members of an audience. I don't use them.

Do's and Don'ts

- **Do** interact with the audience for 15 minutes before a session begins
- **Do** know your audience and design an opening to match their needs
- **Do** identify the purpose and expectations for the session

- **Do** begin on a good note: use mixers and openers
- **Do** honor the expertise of the audience
- **Do** focus on what you have in common with participants
- **Do** make eye contact with members of the audience
- **Do** radiate energy
- **Do** allow the audience to see you
- **Do** look into the eyes of participants
- **Don't** play music that is likely to offend audience members
- **Don't** overwhelm audiences with your accomplishments—share just enough to establish credibility
- **Don't** distance yourself from the audience with comments about lifestyle or experiences not integral to the session purposes

CHAPTER FIVE

Put Teeth Into Your Technique

We must be the change we wish to see . . .

Mahatma Gandhi, 1869–1948

PURPOSE DRIVES PROCESS

Step 1 in planning for any presentation is establishing the goal: the purpose for conducting the training or making the speech. It might be problem solving to cut waste, teaching a software application to an office staff, or motivating employees to work as a team. A strong presenter, when pondering vehicles and tools to use in reaching a session goal, asks, "Will this be the most efficient and effective way to accomplish my purpose?" It sounds obvious, even simplistic. But so often activities are chosen because they're entertaining and crowd pleasers, or stories are told because they're sure to garner a laugh—with no regard to whether they reinforce a theme or message. Activity-driven approaches always disappoint, as presentations driven by anything short of an overarching goal fail. No rubber on the pavement. No traction. No change.

Here's the pearl. Decide what you want to do. Then spend all effort needed to reach that target—that's *process*. Facilitate in a box and set tight parameters that are so carefully planned and orchestrated that failure is nigh impossible. Funnel the audience toward your goal.

As you plan, keep in mind your efforts to bring change to people, and remember change is tough to do. The only way your training will translate into new behavior is if people believe the new information or skills will make their job easier or the quality of their life better. Declaring to an audience, "Trust me," with a glint off your tooth as you say it, won't earn buy-in. You must convince. All activities and every task, therefore, better make clear what is in it for *them*. Start there, always.

- Make abstract concepts concrete and clear—sometimes through stories, perhaps metaphors, maybe visual representations.
- Deliver your presentation dynamically—not only with words, but also with nonverbal communication.
- Touch emotion.
- Guide products, ideas, and skill refinement to align with session content.
- Build in time for reflection.
- Encourage collegial interaction.
- Apply newly acquired skills to personal or professional settings.

Connections, connections. There's something in this for *me*.

QUESTIONS AND ANSWERS

Delivering the Main Course: Information, Skills, and Message

Q: I understand the importance of a message. Should I identify my purpose—my message—in my opening statement?

A: Surely, a general overview as mentioned in Chapter 4 will help. However, the single most effective way to communicate any goal is to *model* it: model the change you are trying to impart to your participants and use the content as the vehicle. If your training topic is the power of group work, then use groups in the process of the session. If you are striving to change attitudes, reflect the attitude and ideas you hope the listeners will accept. Clarity in process serves purpose.

Q: Any tips to connect with the audience when delivering a keynote from a podium?

A: A truly effective technique, although not comfortable for everyone and not appropriate for every situation, is to walk—occasionally—to the front of the stage and speak directly to the audience. The closer you are physically to the audience, the more eye contact you make, the more connected the audience will feel. Remember, this is about buy-in, and there must be connection before the audience buys in. Lean toward the audience and turn to face different segments of the audience. Speak *with* the audience, not *to* the podium.

Limiting Content

Q: My topic is complex, with so much content that time is my enemy.

A: The less on the plate, the more one can chew. In other words, zero in on the most essential components of your message and develop them fully. This was a tough lesson for me to learn—that great quantities of material spread too thinly left audiences confused, frustrated, and unable to process or reflect. Translated, it means audiences walk away with a full menu but no message digested enough to bring change in behavior or performance. Failure results because nothing changes. Tackle only the fundamentals to which you can do justice within the time allotted. If you can't bring to attendees a solid understanding of the message, adequate reflection opportunities, and time for personal application, then you're tackling too much. Lessen the quantity of material or bargain for more time.

Reflections and Connections

Learn to pause . . . or nothing worthwhile will catch up to you.

Doug King

Q: Time's short. Why waste it on reflection and application within a session? Couldn't it be better spent on skill building and content acquisition? It seems like participants could practice and apply on their own time.

A: Half right. The real-life implementation *is* their responsibility, but it is the presenter's job to ensure that participants are *capable* of doing it. I suppose this goes back to hitting our target. To change behavior, adults must understand what you are talking about, agree it has merit, and then see how it relates to and benefits them. Reflection (thinking and talking about) makes application possible (how could I possibly use this?).

Adults learn best in situations that require them to solve problems and integrate learning into real life (Leonard & DeLacey, as cited in Selsor, 2003). Content, no matter how profound, makes little impact on anyone unless that person believes *he or she needs it* for some purpose. Reinforcing heavy content with individual and group interaction ensures that information is covered faster, understood better, and connected to participants' needs. If you simply tell them the important material and expect them to cogitate on its application, you will be sorely disappointed in your effectiveness, even if you're the most charming presenter ever.

Q: I can't build in practice! My standard 45-minute program requires every one of those minutes be spent delivering information. Get real.

A: If a session is longer than 60 minutes, provide at least 2 to 3 minutes for conversation between colleagues—or personal reflection—or compilation of key points in a running journal. If time is shorter, arrange that folks reflect *after* the session ends. Assign a project requiring application of content to be submitted and reviewed by you or the hiring client. The use of postsession evaluations, submitted postsession, is more casual. Ask, "How will your performance be impacted as a result of this training?" or "How will the information or skills be implemented at the work site?" It's a fair expectation—not a formal part of the session, but a mandated extension of training.

Motivating an Audience

Q: How do I get people excited about something they didn't choose to attend? My audiences come because it is mandated by management.

A: Short of explaining the art of fire building to someone stranded in a rustic cabin in January, few audiences are likely hang on your every word just because *you* think the content is interesting.

Everyone in your audience has an agenda. It's your job to get a handle on what that agenda is. I repeat: if participants believe that your message will make their life easier or help them become more efficient, you have their attention. To learn what is needed, use information gleaned from conversations with hiring clients, presession interviews with key players, and conversations with participants before sessions begin. Learn the job descriptions and responsibilities of those in attendance and ask them to identify the hardest part of their job. *Nothing is interesting if you're not interested.*

Figure 5.1

Big Picture

Get the Picture . . . Sometimes seasoned professionals believe they know it all, and resent attending training that promotes any new process or strategy. This activity illustrates the importance of assessing all information before reaching conclusions.

Choose a detailed visual, with variety in texture or color. It might be a photo of a flower bed, a crowd of people, or a city skyline. In advance of the audience's arrival, set up a projection device in the training room—being sure that when turned on, the projected image is immediately and completely *out of focus.* You want participants to see an undecipherable smudge of color and shadows.

When appropriate in the training, ask each person to decide what the image really is. Let them speculate with colleagues and share out a few of the guesses with the whole group. Then continue.

- Focus the image ever so slightly, asking individuals to again speculate as to what it is. Has their idea changed? Why? Share with neighbors and then invite sharing with the whole group.
- Repeat twice.
- Finally, project the image fully focused.

The audience will be amused, amazed, and laughing! Once they settle, comment on the inaccuracies of original guesses. Then get serious:

"Even though you are seasoned individuals, savvy and wise, it is easy to make errors when decisions are made before details are clear. Today is about sharpening our professional pictures–about learning all the pertinent facts, gaining all data, and fitting them into the big picture. Today we work to reach sound conclusions based on a complete and clear picture!"

Now, begin training. Your audience will be much more willing to listen!

Generating New Thinking

Listen long enough and the person will generally come up with an adequate solution.

Mary Kay Ash, founder of Mary Kay
Cosmetics

Q: Is brainstorming the best way to generate new approaches to old problems?

A: Sometimes. Brainstorming, however, doesn't have to be done in groups—consider solo brainstorming. Four people working together generate only about half as many ideas as the combined work of four individuals brainstorming alone. The desire to appear cooperative and reach consensus can cut off the generation of creative new approaches as people rush to conform. Group dynamics can dampen innovation (Smith, Ward, & Schumacher, 1993).

Try variations on brainstorming. Allow individuals to come up with their own creative list and then have groups use the resulting best ideas to refine and develop them further. Another great way to stimulate thinking is by asking everyone to share ideas on their solo brainstorm list with a partner—getting at least one (maybe two) new ideas that have never before been considered. Repeat the process a second and third time. Follow with groups of three to four people prioritizing results and refining the strongest ideas.

Understanding: Taking the Road Less Traveled

Q: No matter how clearly and logically I lay out an argument, many participants misunderstand my message. How can I make sure they get it?

A: Don't rely solely on logic or verbal textbook explanations to help people understand. Few people acquire meaning through auditory input alone and need alternative methods of communication to arrive at an "aha." It may mean comparing the new concept with something generally familiar and understood, noting similarities in form or function (metaphors and analogies). Or it may be telling a story to convince listeners that it doesn't pay to rest on past successes, but work to monitor and meet market needs:

Let me ask the employees of Smith Enterprise, who is the leading retailer today? (Audience responds.) Do you know the leading retailer 50 years ago? (Let 'em guess, they'll likely be wrong.) Then reveal the answer: Corporation X! "In 1955, Corporation X held 83% of market share." Quote X's current market share, and follow with a simple statement: "If Smith Enterprise fails to keep pace with changing times, it could meet the fate of Corporation X—out of date and perhaps out of business. If you're standing still, you're not moving forward. The world continually changes and so must Smith Enterprise."

Chances are, the audience will understand.

Q: I know the effectiveness of analogies, stories, and metaphors. But you also mention nonverbal approaches to increasing understanding. What do they look like?

A: They can take many forms. Let me give you an example that might be appropriate when an audience is resistant to change (i.e., winning buy-in from a veteran audience with the "I'm highly experienced and have all the answers" attitude). Involve participants in a quick task viewing an image—not verbal, not language based.

Audience members are asked to view two figures projected on a screen: "Compare the relative size and shape of these two figures:"

In silence, overlay a transparency atop the left figure and trace the tabletop. Shift and overlay the outline atop the second figure, demonstrating that what *appears* dissimilar is really the same. It blows their minds. One sentence is all it takes: "Sometimes, our experience and perspectives lead us to incorrect conclusions. We need to see through new eyes and consider new possibilities. Today is *about* those new possibilities."

Q: So you accomplish understanding through stories, metaphors, analogies, and visuals?

A: Yes, but it can be done with language, too. Build the need to know with a pretest, questionnaire, or survey that participants complete in 2–3 minutes. The questions should entail key points from the impending session, centering on information that isn't common knowledge. Let them take the test alone and then turn to neighbors to compare (and discuss) similarities and differences in answers. Follow with a whole group debrief of the conversations, but in no case reveal correct answers. Folks become curious and seek to validate or refute their initial answers all through the session.

Figure 5.2

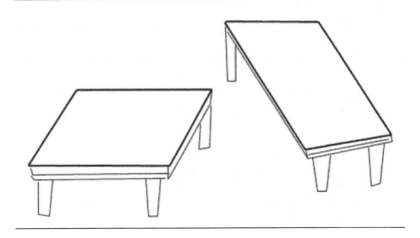

Q: I intuitively use a lot of humor. Is that smart?

A: Humor can be very effective. When folks voice frustration with a difficult process—or perhaps the stubbornness of management or staff to change—I throw up a visual of a man pushing an elephant. It says it all. And with one picture I not only validate their frustration, but demonstrate the difficulty of what we're attempting to accomplish. It's embodied in a lighthearted visual!

> *Once you get people laughing, they're listening and you can tell them almost anything.*
>
> Herbert Gardner

> *To get 'em listening, get 'em laughing.*
>
> Allen Klein

Nonverbal Communication

Q: The topic on which I train is sophisticated and complex, so don't word choice and logic preempt all?

A: No, not really. Of course you want to choose words carefully, being accurate and succinct. But content is only a small part of message efficacy. Communicate *with* an audience; don't talk *at* them. Use your entire body to drive home a point: overview by sledge hammer! In 1967, Albert Mehrabian of UCLA found that only 7% of a message's meaning is determined by the actual words used, whereas 38% is conveyed by the *way* in which the words are spoken—the voice. The most amazing of his revelations is that 55% (most) of the meaning of a message comes from the facial expressions and body language of the speaker. Most social communication is nonverbal (Peoples, 1992). *Energy.*

Q: So it's facial expressions and body language. I do a lot of keynote speaking, and most of my audience can't really see my face. Now what?

A: Both facial expression and body language make a difference. In a small room, look into the eyes of individuals as you speak with them and you'll grab their attention. In a large hall, arrange lighting that illuminates your face. No matter what size audience, give the perception of looking directly at each individual at least once during a session (directing your gaze at every portion of the hall at least once). People will try to catch your eye from that point forward and be far more engaged in personal communication.

And no matter how large the facility, anyone can read body language. Slumped over? Looks like no enthusiasm. Hands on your hips? Not inviting. Look at the floor? Not confident. Stand tall, open your body to face the audience, and connect.

Hand gestures also drive home meaning, making spoken words memorable. In fact, the majority of listeners recall substantially more of what they hear when relevant hand gestures accompany speech, whereas recall declines when a speaker fails to use gestures or hides behind a podium (Bower, 2003).

Q: You talk of nonverbal and nonlinguistic communication to drive home a point. I already use great visuals, such as PowerPoint slides, to display colorful charts with statistics, facts, and quotes. I don't always find them to be so effective. Why?

A: There is probably nothing wrong with your statistics. In fact, there's a need for detail to prove a point or validate a generalization. But the generalized buy-in is what causes participants to pay attention to your statistics! Use visuals, perhaps cartoons or icons with words.

 Build your case through personal and positive connections to the training message. Say I'm working to convince employees to sign up for volunteer refresher courses. I can quote statistics about the increased effectiveness of retrained workers and show graphs displaying actual data regarding the fall-off of productivity as time between training sessions increases. But if I tell a story, well see what you think:

Fred learned that ACME Lumber Company paid its lumberjacks higher wages than did his own employer. Inquiring about job opportunities, he discovered that ACME had no job openings.

Fred, believing he was the best lumberjack in the region, offered ACME a deal they couldn't refuse. He would work without pay to prove his worth; if he could beat ACME's all-time lumbering record of twenty-four felled trees in a single day, he would be hired. If he failed, ACME was under no obligation to him. ACME accepted the wager.

The following day, he arrived early and worked like a demon. Never stopping, he ended the day exhausted—but certain his goal had been reached—until the trees were counted. Only 21! In disbelief, he requested another chance, which was quickly granted.

The lad arrived the next morning, rested, robust, and determined. But at day's end, the count revealed only 19 downed trees. The young man looked the foreman in the eye, saying, "I'm not the man I thought I was. I don't deserve the job."

The older man caught his shoulder and turned to look him square in the eye. "Son," he said. "How long has it been since you sharpened your axe?"

Bypass the intellectual process initially, which can cause learners to scour statistics and argue with facts, and use emotion instead. Then, *after* you've gained attention and general understanding, share data and statistics that provide analytical proof. The audience is then apt to give full consideration to the logic of your presentation.

Q: Why the emotional hook first and the statistics last? Shouldn't I make and prove the argument first, then summarize with nonverbals?

A: No. Human brains need the big picture before they fill in the details. It's a little like putting together a 500-piece jigsaw puzzle.

Do you open the box, take out a single piece, and search for another one that fits next to it? No. You first look at the picture on the puzzle box top! Then you understand what you're trying to create and can tackle the components—the pieces—and tediously assemble them to produce the whole. We view drawings before we assemble a child's wagon, and we request a project example before starting an academic assignment. Big pictures first, details last.

Small Groups to Enliven Learning

Q: How can I prevent reflection time from becoming dead time (yawn)?

A: Remember the purpose of reflection is to force review or application of content, not to force solitude! Try techniques that demand interaction, like buzz groups of no more than three to four colleagues. Ask each group to select a recorder to capture ideas generated. Give clear task directions regarding what to discuss or what product to create (i.e., generate three possibilities, a professional application, the two most . . .). Ask the group to reach consensus on the product. Set a specified time for the task, and let them go. Then discuss results with the whole audience.

Q: Sounds great, but my audiences are fairly large and could require ten groups of four—so it's cumbersome to share products from small groups. Should I skip the debrief?

A: When task time ends, call all attention back to you. Re-allot time for one additional group task: to prioritize to determine the top three ideas on their list for discussion with the entire audience. Ask a spokesperson from each group to share the group's highest priority idea not already contributed by another group. Record the group shared information on an overhead or chart (depends on group size), reserving discussion and judgment. After all contributions are made, view the list and lead a discussion on the merits or possibilities of ideas listed. There is no duplication and no wasted time.

If there are more than ten groups in the facilitation, add one more step to make the task more manageable. After small groups finish their work, use a pyramid approach for production and prioritizing. Ask two groups to join and discuss their individual priorities to reach consensus as to the three best ideas within the second, combined group. A smaller number of large groups then reports for recording and subsequent discussion.

Timing Group Work

Q: How do I gauge the amount of time for a task? I either allot too little or too much!

A: Yes, either can cause trouble. Too little either frustrates or angers people because they can't produce a decent product in the time provided, and too much brings on a whole lot of restroom breaks (from which folks aren't always inclined to return). Here's a solution: if the product is a fairly easy one to complete, provide 2–3 minutes at most. If there is a more demanding task at hand, give 5 minutes—and warn the groups when the time is half up: "Time is half up—you'll want to invite participation from those who haven't yet had an opportunity to contribute." That way, groups work more efficiently. Plus it reduces the likelihood that extroverts will dominate time in a short work period.

Maintaining Involvement

Q: What is to stop folks from taking the restroom breaks? Isn't group work just a signal to get up and relax?

A: I sure hope not! Remember, if there is a product assigned and you make clear that every member is accountable for the product, you will have much more interest from individuals to participate—and see the task through to completion.

Q: This time thing bothers me. Even if groups are efficient, they aren't always done with their task assignment when time expires. Talk about angry and frustrated—should I monitor and let them continue until finished, even if time's expired?

A: Reconvene *exactly* when you said you would. Ask if a little more time might help them polish their products—they'll be grateful that you noticed—and *then* allocate a new amount of time and let them resume. Never just extend the time without stopping and reconvening. If you do, groups won't take time limits seriously during the next task, and they'll begin wasting time, taking breaks, and all the other stuff that turns your hair gray.

Regaining Attention

Q: How do you regain control of the entire group when time expires? People sometimes ignore me, and the old flash-the-lights routine is not always possible—not to mention somewhat trite.

A: Use the old directions-up-front technique, where the group practices *how* to refocus attention a time or two before beginning the day's first group task. I usually just use my arms over my head while using my voice: "Can we recollect our attention up front?" Then, pause briefly and provide the opportunity for groups to oblige. If they respond too slowly, when attention *is* finally regained I reexplain the process, and we once more practice a time or two to get it right. This is always done with a humorous overtone and a clear understanding that it is needed to save time and avoid chaos. In addition to voice and signals, funny whistles, signs, and music are great cues. As long as any technique is clearly explained, practiced a time or two and used consistently, it'll work.

Ensuring Active Participation

Q: How do I get volunteers for activities so that everyone participates—there are individuals who would die before speaking on behalf of a group!

A: I do understand, and if the presenter is familiar with the personalities of the audience, he or she may choose to avoid putting individuals on the spot (as I did by having groups choose their own spokespersons). The problem arises when those not chosen to speak feel excused (in their mind) from contributing to, refining, and communicating the product. Change and growth require each person to be accountable, although it must be accomplished safely and without threat.

Here's one way. After groups complete their task and reconvene to the entire audience, assign one more (timed) task: "You have 1.5 minutes to ensure that every member of your group knows and can clearly state the answers or products of the group." Once done, it's fair game to randomly select anyone to speak for their group.

Q: How do you "randomly" select?

A: Do something lighthearted and unexpected—the person with the longest pinky finger, lightest colored shoes, longest commute to work, and so forth. Spin a spinner or pick a number from a hat—just be sure to keep the qualifiers gender neutral and never off-color. Also, a nice twist might be fun: once a person is identified (longest pinkie?), ask them to point to the person in the group who will be the spokesperson!

Q: What if there is need for one volunteer from the audience at large? I've pleaded at times for help, to no avail. And assigning someone to the job is just deadly!

A: If no one volunteers, I spontaneously use "pick 'em" slips. It's a bundle of five paper slips (a standard supply I carry in the transparency box, along with my markers, tissue, and so on, so it is available at the drop of a hat) that I pass out randomly to scattered members of the audience. I direct them to leave the slip closed until instructed to open it. The slips are numbered, and the messages on each are sequenced to read:

Figure 5.3

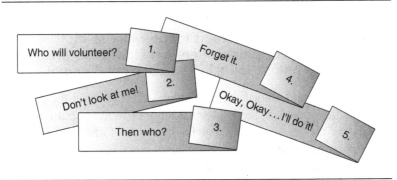

Note, again I revert to a random and lighthearted approach, hedged always by asking Person 5, "Would you do this for us?" I've never been refused participation, but have sensed discomfort. If that happens, look for participants to come to your aid who are seated immediately around the reluctant winner—there will be plenty of volunteers. People like to win.

Tight Parameters to Ensure Success

(Facilitate in a box and then trust your audience to climb out)

Q: When I'm moving quickly through an activity, how can I be sure everyone understands directions? It drives me crazy when folks look at me halfway through a task with furrowed brow and ask, "What were we supposed to do?"

A: You're right to be annoyed—you can't run smoothly and efficiently if confusion interrupts the process. Whenever I give instructions for a task, whether simple or complex, I *write directions down* and leave them projected while the task is being tackled. Folks are highly visual (usually), so it helps it all register. Plus it gives a point of reference for staying on track.

Q: Sometimes it's not a question of understanding—it's a discussion of attitude!

A: Both understanding and acceptance can be verified in several ways. Looking directly into the eyes of audience members (remember, if you want people to look at you, look directly at them) until they make eye contact with you. Ask them to nod if they understand (agree in concept) with what you are asking them to do. Then, scan the entire group to make it appear that each eye is engaged. Once you see uniform nods, say "OK" and go forward. A variation on this is for use with ideas for which buy-in is essential (such as reaching consensus in a strategic planning facilitation). Ask individuals to face you so that no one but you can see their chest. Instruct them to put their forearm and fist directly against their chest, and display either a thumb up or down to reflect their willingness to accept an idea. Again, scan the entire audience, and if you see thumbs down, go back to the drawing board after indicating a failure to reach consensus (but under no circumstances indicate whose or how many thumbs-down there were).

Q: Back up. What if there are thumbs down, what then?

A: Announce that there still exists some reluctance among participants. Pause and ask what it would take to get folks to agree to or feel a level of comfort with an idea. Folks are usually willing to identify the tweaks needed to enable them to reach consensus—without entering into a diatribe or lobbying for a cause. It is a great way to quickly—and publicly—help folks change wording to find common ground. If real controversy still exists and it cannot be overcome with minor changes, return to small workgroups to allow further editing. Step back to consider a whole new array of possibilities.

Q: When I use small groups for interactive tasks, my training often turns into chaos. Any sure-fire suggestions to avoid that?

A: Whenever I use group work for informal, spontaneous tasks, I follow three rules.

1. Always time tasks. If you don't, you'll have some groups working and others lollygagging, plus folks feeling they can take personal breaks. Make the time allotment slightly less than you think even the fastest group would need: believe me, they *will be* on task!

2. Assign a product the group must complete.

3. Make each individual accountable. If you use random methods of choosing a group spokesperson, then provide ample extra minutes before the selection to ensure that all group members are on board, informed, and ready to serve as spokesperson. Or after the random selection, provide a few moments for the entire group to counsel and prepare the spokesperson to speak for the entire group. When folks realize they represent or are responsible for the group as a whole, they feel a sense of responsibility and accountability. And there *will be* fewer unscheduled bathroom breaks!

It works.

DO'S AND DON'TS

- **Do** identify purpose for the session first, and then let process and activities derive from it
- **Do** gain audience buy-in, making sure there is value for all
- **Do** make eye contact with the audience

- **Do** check for understanding
- **Do** ensure full participation
- **Do** occasionally brainstorm solo
- **Do** use humor and a lighthearted approach
- **Do** concentrate on nonverbal communication: it has more impact than what we say!
- **Do** use stories and metaphors; they can drive home points more effectively than statistics!
- **Do** build in time for individual and group reflection
- **Do** set rigid rules for group work: time, product, and accountability
- **Don't** forget to make attendees apply their learning
- **Don't** separate yourself physically from the audience
- **Don't** leave anything to chance!

CHAPTER SIX

Enthrall 'em All

JOB 1: MAKE TIME DISAPPEAR

Some presenters seem to be magic. Must be born with it, eh? Now, I'll admit that some personalities connect with audiences easier than others. But variety in style and personality is as important a spice in presenting as it is in life. And thankfully, even the average bear can learn techniques that make for skilled speaking and training. The difference between a dynamite person doing a mediocre job and a mediocre person doing a dynamite job is technique. And we aren't born with that.

Success is not the result of spontaneous combustion.

You must first set yourself on fire.

Fred Shero

INFUSING EXCITEMENT INTO SESSIONS

Basic #1: **People loathe monotony**—in anything. Movies, voices, scenery. Love shrimp? After three straight meals of it, you crave a slab of meatloaf. Swoon while listening to a favorite recording artist? Ten repeats of the same song track, you'll wing the CD out a window. Talk, talk, talk? Give me silence. Too much silence? Somebody make a sound! Any static aspect of our lives brings an ache for change, and everybody needs it—I mean, with swimming pools and yachts out his backdoor, ever wonder why even John D. Rockefeller needed a vacation?

The only difference between a rut and a grave is the depth of the hole.

Roland Barth (1990)

Use this knowledge to be a savvy presenter. To capture and enthrall the audience, recognize that folks want—no, *need*—change: of state, of context, of activity. There's nothing wrong with lecture, but it better be broken up with tasks that involve activity and involvement. Group tasks fun? Yep, but better not continue indefinitely or people will want to scream from the frenetic monotony of them. Giving breaks is easy. The dilemma is providing embedded activities that bring changes of state that are *true to session goals*. Rehooking an audience boils down to weaving meaningful novelty, via energy and movement, into process. The goal is a rapt audience, eager and focused. Note these adjectives all have positive connotations: keeping the crew happy makes the boat go.

VARIETY AS A VEHICLE

Basic #2: **Use variety and stimulation *as vehicles*** for engaging and maintaining audience attention, *not* as avenues of entertainment. Infuse them into process. They should *not* stand alone, as in a performance, but serve to help audiences understand, connect with, and rehearse session content. Even voice should be used skillfully. Changes in pitch, volume, and timbre keep listeners engaged: a pause draws attention to a profound statement that follows, and inserted seconds of silence give the listener time for reflection. Try taping your voice to practice more effective delivery.

Change pace of speech *and* of activity. In the midst of break-speed activity, slip in brief periods of calm reflection or notation. It's powerful. Conversely, extended sedentary stretches need occasional inserts of quick exchange between colleagues. "Turn to your neighbor and tell them what you heard."

MONITORING AN AUDIENCE

Basic #3: **Look at your audience!** Study your audience continuously to spot spikes and drop-offs in engagement and enthusiasm. *Skilled* presenters read the audience for indicators of disengagement, and when fatigue or boredom is spotted, they shift gears instantaneously

Figure 6.1

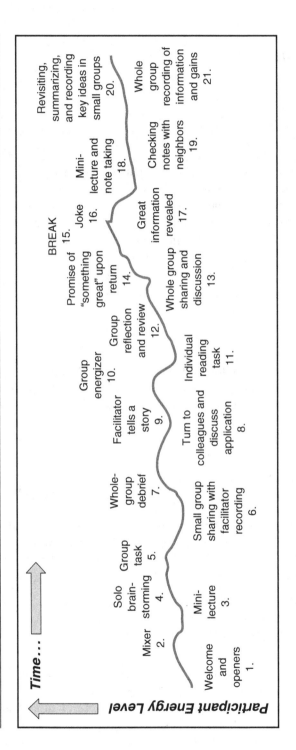

to recapture their audience. Peaks and plateaus! Every dip demands a change of state to rebuild energy and pull the audience back up. Never let an audience hit bottom. Avoid extreme peaks and valleys. Tapping folks back on track when they veer is easy—hoisting them from the bottom is tough. Keep an eye on that audience. Even a hiker can't see the mountains if he's looking at his feet.

> *It's amazing what you can observe just by watching.*
>
> Yogi Berra

The 1–2–3 Rule

Basic #4: **Follow the 1–2–3 rule** when working with training sessions. If one participant leaves the room during the session, ignore it. Two: pay attention. Three? Break immediately—your audience needs a restroom stretch. And in the case of audience attention, same rule: if one person's eyes roll back into their head *and* they drool, figure they were up late with a new baby. Two people doing it? Be suspicious. Three? *Change state.* By the way, after lunch it's okay to go directly from 1 to 3 in the rulebook. It's doubtful that *any* audience, even with appropriate changes of state, can last more than 60 minutes at that time of day. Provide an energizer no more than 30 minutes into the segment and as many other subtle changes of state appropriate to your purpose within that after-lunch hour. In addition, at the end of the hour, provide participants a formal break to stretch their legs. If you don't let them, they'll do it anyway. And be mad at *you* for not thinking of it first. Feed 'em, move 'em, and break 'em.

Questions and Answers

Introductions Set the Tone

Q: So does this happy energy thing start right away? I thought you encouraged immediate introductions and overviews.

A: I do! Participant introductions at session opening establish safety and a sense of community that last the whole presentation. Since facilitations require professional interaction and decision making, trust and respect between participants is paramount. Help individuals make personal connections and establish common ground with other attendees. People love permission to talk about themselves, so give it to them by mandating they do it in a task. But beware: introductions should quickly set a positive tone, so solicit only constructive thoughts. What do you hope to gain from this day? What is the biggest contribution you can make to the success of this session? What is your main interest regarding this topic?

Q: Rarely do all attendees take introductions seriously. They sit with their friends, so is there any point to introductions?

A: When possible, ask people to introduce themselves to someone they know very little or not at all. Or ask folks to find a partner for this task at another table or in another part of the room. What you don't want to do is upset their comfort level right off the bat by mandating a *permanent* change of location. After introductions are complete, allow people to return to their original seats.

Q: Is an introductory activity needed if everyone knows everyone else?

A: If participants do know each other, choose tasks that build esprit de corps. Perhaps instruct folks to cluster with all others in the group who share their favorite flavor of ice cream, enjoy similar vacation destinations, or were born in the same place. Colleagues will learn new things about their old friends—laughing and moving in the process—to begin a session that recognizes *similarities exist between all people*. It can be a powerful way to relax a crowd prior to laboring on tedious tasks and joins people who ordinarily choose not to mix.

Change of State

Q: Do I have to provide changes of state if my audience looks engaged? Is the rule of thumb to change activities when they look antsy?

A: To keep folks engaged, don't let more than 20 minutes pass without a change of state. Oh, shrewd participants can sit and *look* attentive for up to 90 minutes, but they likely won't easily learn or retain what's being presented. Folks can look you right in the eye, yet be thinking about lunch or what time the kids are done at soccer.

Directly and actively involve individuals in content every 8 minutes or so. Does that apply to a 45-minute keynote? You bet. Any skilled communicator will find a catalyst for physical reaction from the audience to break the monotony of continuous listening: a story that draws sighs or comment between audience members, humor that brings guffaws or belly laughing, or emotion that pulls a visceral response.

Q: You say to involve folks in content every 8 minutes or so. I'll never get anything done if I have to stop every 8 minutes!

A: Don't take me too literally (like the person who set a kitchen timer to ring every 8 minutes. Talk about breaking focus! The audience ended up watching the clock so they could warn her when the timer was about to go off). The trick is to make the transitions seamless, with one segment flowing into the next. The changes can be subtle (and usually are): *Summarize what you just heard and share it with the person either in front or behind you, Jot this down, Reflect on related material in a handout, Check your neighbor's notes to ensure all information was recorded.* Then, resume the original task.

Q: So we're talking about cycling from lecture to mini-breaks for conversation or reflection?

A: It's more than that. It involves changes in several aspects of a task:

T-I-E: Time, Interaction, and Energy

- The *time* allotted, from extended periods for measured group or individual reflection to short tasks demanding speedy completion for spontaneous output
- The degree of *interaction*, from individual to small group to whole group
- The amount of the *energy* spent by participants, from sedentary to active

Movement: More Than a Sign of Life, the Glue for Learning

Q: It sounds like you want people moving much of the time. Don't adults prefer to sit still and be left alone?

A: No, they don't. If they're under 40 years of age, folks are chompin' at the bit to do something. And if they're over 40, their knees lock up if you don't let them move once in a while! Seriously, nobody needs (or wants) to be moving all the time (remember, variety). But there's great benefit to building movement into session activities whenever possible—especially during slump times and right before lunch. Here's why (this is serious stuff).

Brains operate electrochemically. Brain nerve cells (neurons) communicate via neural circuits to both create and recall memories. Brain chemicals (neurotransmitters) activate neurons to fire those neural circuits. There are many different brain chemicals, each with specific and multiple functions. One, acetylcholine, is involved in conscious movement, but *also* is an enabler of something called long-term potentiation (LTP). In essence, LTP equates to planting memory. Now this is key: each time there is physical movement, acetylcholine is released in the brain. This increased presence of acetylcholine makes it is easier for a brain to plant and retrieve memory. So movement may actually enhance learning: not just for kinesthetic people, but all people! Energizers have real value.

Energizers

Q: Are energizers synonymous with changes of state?

A: They're one type of change. Energizers serve a different purpose than process changes (T-I-Es). Those, remember, help the brain reengage *with content*. Energizers help the body *and* brain avoid fatigue: they recharge, refocus, and ready audiences to continue (so reengagement is possible). Unlike changes of state, which relate to content activity, energizers can be stand-alone activities inserted midstream when fatigue starts but agenda breaks are impossible to give. Some examples are to provide an 11-second stretch for audience members to rise and move to direction (maybe to music); pause and tell a joke; ask a series of questions that are answered in the negative by sitting and in the positive by standing, so that participants are physically active; give 38-second "tag breaks" when individuals must locate a person further than 10 feet away and jointly answer some question.

Q: So energizers occur somewhere within a long segment?

A: Often, yes. But if your audience has been sitting for 45 minutes or more before you get them, do an energizer immediately—before the start of your segment! Audience members will then be ready to engage and focus on your material. Also, note that if proper T-I-Es (changes of state) are embedded in the process and timely breaks are provided, energizers may not be necessary.

Figure 6.2

Energizers

√ Keep 'em short (1–3 minutes)
√ Consider using music to signal starts and stops, with selections that reflect the desired tone of the activity
√ Give clear, concise directions
√ Plug 'em into slump times—especially about 30 to 35 minutes after lunch

A. Stand Up If: A great way to take a break when you don't have time for a real one! This can even be done in theater-style seating. It is easy to build in a little review of content and intersperse it with humor along the way! In a quick-paced fashion, instruct participants to stand, and then immediately sit back down, as a positive response to questions like these:
Stand Up If You

1. Understand this stuff . . .
2. Know one way to . . .
3. Want to extend this training, as you're really on a roll and don't want to stop now!
4. Get an increased work load 'cause you're sooo efficient!
5. Believe we CAN improve!
6. Plan on stopping back at the office tonight, just to make sure all loose ends are tied up . . .
7. Wish the word "compliance" had never been coined!
8. Love your boss to invite the company CEO to "drop in on *you* anytime!"
9. Oh heck—stand up if you're ready to take a break!"

B. Bag 'O Jokes: Keep it on hand at all times. When attention or energy lags, have someone reach into the bag and read one to the group. Invite the group to give a thumbs up or down to the joke.

C. Peer Sharing: After lecturing for 20 minutes or following any tedious, sedentary and ongoing activity, choose an energizer appropriate to the time you can afford and the space in which you are working.

   – *Pair-Share:* Takes little time and space. Ask participants to turn to someone either beside, in front of, or behind them and share what they have just heard, or learned, or how to apply content. Allow no more than 1.5 minutes.
   – *Move and Talk:* Takes some room and more time. Ask participants to identify a peer and walk to another part of the room to reflect on the importance of the strategies or information. Combining physical movement with rehearsal both energizes the participants and improves retention. Allow no more than 3 minutes for this energizer.

D. Physical Movement: This is great to not only energize, but help participants get back on track when their thinking is bogged down from tedium. Ask participants to do quick, simple, in-place cross lateral movement:

   – Stand and reach across to opposite sides of their bodies with their arms
   – Pat themselves on their backs, right hand to left side and left hand to right side
   – Cross ankles, cross arms, and stretch upward as far as possible while keeping feet flat on the floor

Breaks

Q: Do energizers substitute for breaks?

A: No. Energizers lift and motivate within a session to eliminate fatigue, whereas breaks give the brain and body a short vacation from the session.

Q: Any tips to get people back from breaks? I hesitate to give many, because some participants don't return on time or at all.

A: First, solve the dribbling-back-in problem. Assign odd durations for breaks. *Never* 15 minutes—it's so routine, people will "wag" it and lollygag in returning. If, however, you say, "Let's see, it's 10:02. We'll reconvene in *exactly* 13 minutes and 27 seconds!" believe me, they'll be eyeing their watches to return on time! Warning: If you promise a restart time, deliver on it exactly. People then know you mean business and will thereafter be prompt. Second, to lure an audience back, preview and promise something of real interest to those present when a session resumes after break: "Immediately after the break, I'm going to let you in on. . . ." "Anyone back on time will receive. . . ." Then deliver.

Q: People can be in the room and even seated, but I still can't get their attention to begin. Any ideas?

A: Music through the sound system is one of the best I've found. Folks respond to it emotionally (be sure you choose something upbeat and with a fast tempo to regain attention *and* build energy levels to begin work anew). The contrast to room and conversation noise will grab attention for the start.

Putting Lecture in Its Place

Q: Back to delivery. Do I avoid lecture at all costs? "Lecture" is treated like a dirty word these days.

A: Not in my dictionary. Sometimes lecture is the most efficient way to deliver information and is welcomed by listeners. When there is a large volume of information that must be shared, lecture can be great stuff—in limited doses. Purpose drives process! Just don't violate Basic #1! Build variety into your delivery.

Q: I do keynote addresses. There's no way to avoid lecture!

A: If the address lasts an hour or less, a lecture format can be most practical. But that doesn't let you off the hook for providing changes of state. Use subtle variations (changes in voice, speed of delivery, and expressive body language) along with smooth insertion of mental breaks for a shrewd delivery. Use humor, stories, or choraled audience responses. A speaker can keep an audience hooked for a full hour—even in a "lecture!"

Q: My presentations are content heavy, and I am accountable for ensuring that my audiences acquire that content. How do I avoid putting everyone to sleep?

A: Don't try to be the source of all information. Lecturing for more than short periods or explaining laboriously will put all but the most dedicated to sleep. Detailed explanations are often best when embedded in responses to audience questions or when clearing up misunderstandings.

And hard as it is to accept, many in your audience might not be highly motivated to attend your session in the first place ("The boss said I had to come" or "My contract mandates annual recertification"). So the trick is to get folks to interact with content on a personal basis, and then reflect and generalize from it through interaction with others.

Covering Volumes of Content: Alternative Methods

Q: You warn against monotonous activities. My training sessions last hours, often multiple days, and cover huge amounts of content. The professional audiences I serve don't want to waste time. Isn't lecture simply more efficient in such trainings?

A: Assuming you want the audience to actually learn something, no! Long periods of lecture are the kiss of death. No matter how nose-to-the-grindstone they are, *all adults need two things*: (1) change and (2) opportunities to reflect and connect material to their own needs.

Figure 6.3

Covering Large
Amounts of Content without
Lecture: Collaborative Learning

Learners who collaborate perform better. Not only does student retention of course content improve, but collaboration reduces stress—and increases enjoyment of learning!*

A. Pair Reading: Use the power of collaboration to enhance understanding, to encourage recall, and to set the stage for whole group discussion. It is a powerful way to ensure that heavy content is covered, pondered, and recorded. Begin by placing participants in pairs, identifying each as either "A" or "B". Instruct them to follow the following sequence of activities:

- Read aloud together all section headings
- Read first paragraph silently, alone
- Person A summarizes content of paragraph
- Person B coaches (listens carefully, corrects errors, spots and fills in omissions, relates content to previous knowledge)
- Rotate roles for each paragraph, until entire text segment is completed
- As a pair, agree on overall meaning of material
  - Fill out a graphic organizer to record information?
  - Answer task content questions?
  - Apply content to a work task?

B. Read, Reflect, Respond: Each person reads content alone, in its entirety. In the margin of the text, they are instructed to react to information by marking passages that recap that which they already know and understand with "RC." Those passages that require some additional thought and reflection should be noted in the margin with "RF" for reflection needed. Those passages that require more information, that are confusing, or that we challenge in our thinking should be marked "RI" for requiring information.

Following individual reading, preidentified collegial pairs share their understandings, observations, reflection needs, and questions. Allow ample time for steps 1 and 2 (at least 5 minutes for pair reflection after individual reading time ends), and then follow up with a whole group debrief and discussion.

---

*Cortright, Collins, Rodenbaugh, DiCarlo (2003).

Q: Sounds great, but how do I provide change and guarantee reflection and connection time for the audience?

A: Here's one way. Rather than you teaching all content, make participants responsible for teaching others. Assign each individual the reading, analyzing, organizing, and presenting of a specified segment of topic material. The task is to teach the material to others within a larger group. When members of the group complete their teaching, all segments of the body of information are explained and discussed—*without you*, the facilitator, *delivering it*. Such a jigsaw technique works to impart content, while providing changes of state and reflection opportunities as well.

Q: How do I run a jigsaw?

A: Break topic content into two to four categories, creating standalone information sources for each category (i.e., written text, Web site(s), video(s), or even mini-presentations). Form small groups with the number of members equal to the number of categories. Assign each group member a number and its corresponding category of information. It's that body of content that each individual is responsible to teach to the remainder of the group. The firsthand acquisition of material becomes a simultaneous process rather than a lockstep, sequential one, as no individual has to experience firsthand every category resource. The individual is responsible to gather, analyze, synthesize, and teach an assigned body of material to colleagues. It's efficient.

Q: Efficient, yes. But will participants learn and understand material as well in a jigsaw as if it was presented in an organized lecture format?

A: Actually, there are benefits that go beyond efficiency. First, individual accountability goes up—attendees become responsible for their own learning! And when individuals become interdependent, a sense of team develops. Second, research shows that when participants say and do (explain and apply) the content (through teaching, application, use), the likelihood of retention is 90%

(Pike, 1994)! Conversely, if learning depends solely on listening (as in a lecture), the likelihood of retention is only 20%. Even if visuals enhance lecture, the likelihood of retaining information rises to only 50%.

Accountability in Group Work

Q: Sounds good, but some people just think they're "above" working in a session. They let others carry the load. What about that?

A: First, when a session shifts to small group activity, develop accountability by forming teams of *interdependent* people. Assign a category of material to only one individual per group for reviewing and teaching. Make him or her fully accountable for the assignment and thus the only source for that information for others in the group. Then the group *collectively* compiles or evaluates the entire body of information. Every person understands that his or her role is integral to group success and is unlikely to step out to call the office or head to the restroom before completing the task. A variation might involve the group itself dividing work for scavenger hunts, for completing charts, or for fleshing templates.

Q: My audience doesn't go for "touchy feely." Will real professionals accept this stuff?

A: As a rule, individuals take assignments seriously and enjoy sharing observations about content. Acting as a conduit for essential information is empowering. Jigsaw is also fast-paced, plus it provides social interaction (which adults enjoy), saves time, and is high energy. Hmmmmm. That TIE goes nicely: timing, interaction, and energy.

Q: How can I feel confident that the person gathering information is thorough? The material and skills taught in my session are critically important.

A: Find a way to debrief and discuss essential content with the entire audience after group work is complete. Shy of giving an assessment to ensure individual understanding, here's what I would do. Ask individuals to join several others and ask them to reach consensus regarding key elements from the information categories, find items that surprised the group, or identify concerns. Circulate and listen to small groups work to provide ample time for full digestion and discussion of information. Once discussion ends, re-collect attention, ask groups to choose spokespersons, and then debrief and record ideas reported out. Open the floor to discussion and provide opportunity for discourse. Clear up misunderstandings and spot holes that need to be plugged with short lectures or explanation. (Note: I always provide written copies of essential categorical information for reference and personal reference after the activity ends. Adults want their "own copy.")

Group Size

Q: Why do you continually specify groups made up of two to four individuals when you use spontaneous and informal groups?

A: Back to research. Pairs working together experience a 6% increase in achievement over working alone. The increase jumps to 9% in groups of three and four! Surprisingly, groups larger than four actually see achievement drop by about 1% (Marzano, Pickering, & Pollock, 2001). Is that a lot? No. But unless a technique has positive results, avoid using it. Although this research centered on youngsters, my observations of adults bear out the results: keep informal workgroups smaller than five.

Visuals to Enhance Meaning

Q: If visuals enhance comprehension, should I intersperse words with them?

A: Visuals do enhance messages, but choose a format conducive to your message, especially in charts and graphs. Form alters impact. Cartoons, pictographs, and icons sometimes drive home a point better than words, and visual simplicity communicates better than an overload of detail. Choose carefully the best visual to drive home the point you are trying to make. Note the difference:

Figure 6.4

Compare the Impact of These Messages . . .

Likelihood of Comprehension

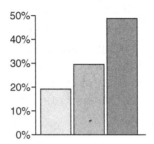

Likelihood of Comprehension

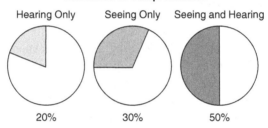

Hearing Only   Seeing Only   Seeing and Hearing

20%   30%   50%

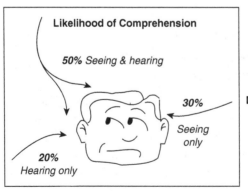

Q: I use great visuals. But when I project a slide, folks barge ahead to copy the words rather than listening and taking notes on each single point.

A: Don't project a series of ideas on one slide. Either limit each slide to one idea or reveal each item one by one, as you discuss it. Keep items on overhead transparencies covered with a sheet of paper or reveal points sequentially by using the slide-build feature of PowerPoint. That way, folks wait for your explanation regarding a single point and can't jump ahead.

Directing Attention

Q: At times, audiences seem unfocused when I use props and charts. What do you suggest?

A: Participants follow the presenter's eyes, so if you want them to view or study a chart, look at it yourself.

Applying Content

Q: How can I help people apply content?

A: Provide time for folks to work solo, in pairs or in small groups to reflect on information after any whole-audience debrief or sharing session. This allows individuals to apply concepts or skills to their specific job responsibilities. It's amazing how many new approaches and strategies are discovered as peers share ideas, make observations, question, and explain to one another. Ideally, each person should walk away with at least one promising possibility. Content, no matter how profound, makes little impact unless there's "something in it for me."

Handling Questions

Q: Are question-and-answer sessions best handled at the end of the day?

A: Questions can be answered throughout a session, in debriefing and reporting sessions, as one circulates listening to small groups work or in formal segments designated for answering concerns. Invite personal questions to be written on small sticky notes and placed on a "question board." This saves time and interruptions during training and allows the facilitator to gather questions during breaks and weave answers into activities and time slots when the session reconvenes. If there is a personal question with no appeal to the audience at large, the facilitator can speak alone with the questioner without spending the whole group's time. When time is short or questions aren't entirely relevant to the session purpose, request they be sent to you via e-mail for detailed answers. Then, answer those sent. This eliminates the riff-raff, casual questions. Nine out of ten folks never go to the trouble of e-mailing, but feel satisfied that had they, you would have responded.

Q: How do I avoid having my presentation interrupted by questions, without seeming rude?

A: Acknowledge in some nonverbal way that you are aware of a hand up or that there is a question—perhaps nodding toward questioners or giving a thumb or hand up toward them—and then finish your thought before responding.

Q: It bothers me that I will be misquoted when answering controversial questions.

A: When asked a question on a touchy issue, answer the question in front of everyone (not alone with one person) so it's less likely to be taken out of context. The key is to seem accessible and interested in meeting concerns and then finding a way to do it smartly and efficiently. If the question is too touchy, it's fine to politely bow out of an answer ("I don't feel I'm in a position to answer that").

Do's AND Don'ts

- **Do** avoid monotony
- **Do** build time for participants to reflect on content
- **Do** keep participant interaction and partnered activities focused and short: 1 to 3 minutes with rare exception
- **Do** make participants move—subtly or overtly—throughout any presentation
- **Do** provide time for participants to apply new information to their jobs or lives

- **Do** look where you want the audience to look—they'll follow your eyes!
- **Do** open a session with an energizer if your audience has been seated for a time
- **Do** give breaks with weird lengths
- **Do** make promises to get folks back—and the last break has the biggest promise
- **Do** use music to signal the restart of a session after break and regain high attention levels
- **Don't** jam slides or overheads with too much detail
- **Don't** let participant energy levels fall and stay off. Observe and react!
- **Don't** fail to give breaks at least every 90 minutes

CHAPTER SEVEN

Rave Reviews

*Making Sure You Still
Have an Audience
Left After Break*

APPEAL

When folks are caught up in activities and time clips along, half the battle's won. Think about it: if the audience is enthralled, it's because they're tuned in. And people stay tuned in when they want more. We've already addressed the importance of building audience rapport, but this chapter describes the icing on the cake of happy campers—qualities and features to keep folks comin' back. Often presenters think it's about *us,* but it's not. It's about *them.* It relates to how we make our *audience* members feel, and that comes from the Big 4 Factors: fun, comfort, mystery, and finesse.

FUN

When choosing between a good time or a stick in the eye, it's an easy choice. Although half the time people don't attend sessions enthusiastically, it's our responsibility to make them glad they did and not wishing they had chosen the stick in the eye. To play on an old adage, "If the audience ain't happy, ain't nobody happy." Nothing's worse than a crabby audience (well, ornery teenage kids might be the exception), because they'll dig in their heels like mules and refuse both change and cooperation with you. That last one can leave you weeping.

Approach things without rancor. Use humor or cast positive light on all that's done. Humans tend to gravitate to those who make them feel good about themselves, so if you want an audience to join you mentally or physically, you'll accomplish it a lot easier if they feel good about the journey. Adults love stories, interactive tasks, fast-paced games, and contests that yield prizes. All are positive, as long as they are part of a medley of tasks and they don't create animosity or too serious competition. And remember, jokes are funnier, stories more profound, and activities more fun when people are clustered to produce group energy.

Notice that movement creeps in again and again? One sure-fire way to guarantee complaints is to keep participants sedentary. One sure-fire way to keep people content is with movement. We have already seen that physical activity—movement—plays a role in creating optimal learning conditions for the brain, increasing levels of alertness, mental function, and learning. Exercise increases blood flow to the brain, but it also releases endorphins, which positively impact mood (Wolfe et al., 2000). Want folks to feel good? That's one more reason to keep them moving.

COMFORT

Comfort can be a physical state—and yes, do whatever is in your power to ensure the room is airy, light, and moderate in temperature (even though the lady in the front row complains about the chill, the fellow in the back will be too hot). But the real nitty-gritty is *emotional* comfort—honoring all learning styles and ensuring safe participation. That means safety to contribute and take risks in pursuit of learning. Build in anonymity, provide feedback, invite revision, and orchestrate interdependence.

MYSTERY

Build intrigue into a presentation, rather than revealing every detail of what's ahead. We *want* a curious audience, as curiosity guarantees attention. We love speculation as it generates effort to find truth. Ask a question, but don't provide an immediate answer. Display materials, but don't rush to explain their use. Tease the audience with promises of the single greatest secret to success, but let the secret unfold gradually. In Chapter 6, we used intrigue to lure folks back from breaks on time. Important information was promised for those who returned promptly and revealed to only those who did. Try also leaving a few handouts out of the formal packet and distributing them only as they are used. Doing it builds interest and grabs attention, creating a change of state as participants pick up materials. And there's an added bonus; it stops participants reading ahead or doing an activity before it's time. The inside scoop? Don't expose all your premises or key elements and don't give away your tricks, or show your props, or display all your charts, or reveal every plan, or provide all materials, or distribute every handout—try unveiling them as you go.

And keynote speakers, unveil *yourself.* Even though you greet members of the audience as they enter, exit the room at least 3–5 minutes before your speech begins. Enter anew when introduced—for drama!

FINESSE

Bottom line, we deal with humans and can't head off *every* possible problem. Perhaps a professional issue such as an unresolved labor dispute throws a monkey wrench into the training environment—sometimes trouble starts with the personality quirk of one attendee. Yet whether the uncomfortable situation involves one flaming . . . uhhh, stinker . . . or a whole room full of them, the result is the same. You can't move forward or backward without dealing with the issue at hand.

Discussions with the hiring client provided insights as to the receptiveness of your audience, which is helpful during planning. But important details that can affect the receptiveness of the audience can be concealed and are not available prior to the start of your session. Use the information you pick up in presession conversations with participants to more accurately gauge an audience's attitude. If you uncover a general concern or discover a glaring issue, address it—even if only with a casual comment. If the concern relates to the day's topic, mention—quickly, briefly, and positively—how the content connects to their concerns.

This chapter establishes the importance of good audience relations. The glue—the final finesse—is when folks, regardless of their issues, can identify *with you.* Personal stories are great, but must demonstrate concerns and feelings shared by the audience. "I served, as have so many of you . . ." or "I remember experiencing the same difficulty in . . ." or "Just like you, I've attended. . . ." Connections are important, but through them must run a thread common to the listener. A story told, a conversation, an experience shared take on importance only when they resonate in our minds and memories. No soldier in combat wants a commander who has only experienced war sitting behind a desk. Winning them over? Make the audience believe the presenter is "one of us."

QUESTIONS AND ANSWERS

When You Don't Have the Answer

Q: Working with complex issues, I have many sophisticated questions asked of me. I live in mortal fear of not knowing something and then losing an audience.

A: If you are at a loss, say so, and then offer to get an answer and contact that person to deliver. Next time, you'll be able to answer that question. If you make an error, whether you or a participant spots it, admit the mistake and humbly move on. People forgive and accept humility—they pounce on and attack bluffers.

Building Fun Into Learning

Q: How can I use movement in a training task? I want tasks that are not only enjoyable, but valuable.

A: Try traveling cards. Provide two questions (A and B) to participants, asking them to write one on each side of a blank half sheet of paper. Structure the task with these guidelines:

- "When I ask you to begin, please respond quickly to the questions on the front and back of your sheet. Make responses legible, but make no identifying marks on your paper."
- "Music will be the signal for you to stop writing and begin circulating around the room."
- "Exchange your paper as you circulate, as many times and with as many people as possible: DO NOT read the sheets!
- "When the music stops, freeze in your tracks and wait for instruction."

Play music that is upbeat and fast-paced, for about 30–60 seconds. People should be "grooving" and smiling throughout this activity.

When the music stops announce, "Locate the person who is physically closest to you, and face them." Then continue with instructions:

- "Read what is written on the paper you hold."
- "Share the responses and your thoughts about them with your partner."

Then, let them begin. You can also frame discussion by instructing pairs to perform specific tasks during conversation (such as determining whether responses are sound or whether they reflect faulty thinking). Circulate and listen during these conversations, before calling full group attention back to you for reflections, observations, and discussion of outstanding points. You'll get quite a discussion and even dialogue between peer pairs.

Q: OK, it's fun and interactive. But does it have a place in a serious training session?

A: Sure it does. The facilitator tailors the task to serve his or her purpose. If that purpose is review of information, original questions will require demonstration of session content. If practice in skill or content application is the goal, questions demand application in professional settings. If the session is a facilitated planning, questions solicit brainstormed possibilities. And if a topic is sensitive, the anonymity of responses promotes an open forum for discussion of controversial ideas without fear of repercussion.

Q: Don't some adults resent games?

A: Not if they are productive and fruitful. Think about this: people are able to move (with purpose), be socially active (which they love), and be involved 100% even if they are introverts (no choosing partners, pairing is random). Also, each person is trapped—*actively* involved with content. No one is on the sidelines.

Q: How about reluctance to discuss openly with someone you may not even know?

A: That's part of the beauty! Each person potentially does converse with a stranger, but the ideas they discuss are contributed anonymously.

They can reflect, critique, and argue safely because there is no personality attached to the ideas. This is a great way to hash and discuss new possibilities, ingenious approaches, or controversial issues safely, comfortably, and without fear of offending.

Q: One problem I encounter is people starting before I'm even done giving instructions. It drives me crazy!

A: Always preface your instructions with the request, "Please don't act on these instructions until I tell you to begin." If you see somebody jumping the gun, repeat the request. It's amazing how people oblige.

Q: Is the use of music a good thing or does it aggravate people?

A: If you are comfortable using music, it is a great addition to presentations. Tempo should match the energy level you want in participants, so calming music is great for the start of the day or the onset of breaks. Fast paced, upbeat music energizes audiences and is great for restoring energy levels as people return from breaks and lunch hours or are departing for the day. Lyrics are fine when music is an energizer—my favorites send messages that reinforce positive feelings ("Don't Worry, Be Happy!"). I have also observed that genre matters (see Chapter 4). Although many trainers use music during extended small group activity, I find its use more of a distraction than a help, particularly if you have an abundance of auditory learners in the session.

Q: You encourage humor, but it's tough to find something universally appealing.

A: Jokes and humor add interest and fun—and the key to appeal is to stay simple and nonoffensive. NEVER do anything off color (I mean anything), demeaning, or politically explosive. You'd have to hold my feet in the fire before I would allude to any political position in a presentation. You may think you know how everyone feels, but believe me you don't. The most credible professionals lose credibility if they are on the wrong side of politics, and the wrong side is whatever the listener disagrees with. Unless an issue is integral to your purpose and its accomplishment, stay away.

Creating Physical and Emotional Comfort

Q: You speak of physical comfort. Hey—I don't own the facility, and I can't control this stuff!

A: Maybe, but you can make folks think you're trying. If the room is blazing hot or too cold to be comfortable, talk to the building management to make adjustments in presession preparations. Then mention early in the session your awareness of the tough conditions, and tell them you have tried to rectify it. In longer sessions, where climate conditions change continually, try this. Display a *comfort board* with various category divisions:

Figure 7.1

Comfort Board
Room Temperature
Lighting
Volume and Sound
Other Concerns?

Invite participants to voice any concerns relating to comfort that arise during the day, by sticking Post-it notes on the board. Assign a volunteer to monitor concerns about lighting, the sound system and levels of volume, room temperature, and so on. This empowers participants and respects their physical needs, yet avoids gripes that might color a session. The audience knows you care, even if you really can't do much beyond notifying management regarding participant concerns.

Q: Sometimes audiences get feisty when required to work intensely for long periods. I change states and activities yet they still act ornery!

A: Give breaks (do I sound like a broken record?). Read your audience continuously to spot agitation, frustration, lack of focus, fatigue, or restlessness. It's better to have frequent, short breaks than one too long that makes it tough to reengage participants. I always feel great when an evaluation says, "Thanks for letting us break so often. It helped me stay tuned-in the whole day!"

Q: Don't many adults prefer to be left alone—not involved in group activities?

A: A common fallacy. There are two pieces of research to refute that: my own via observation of active involvement of adults, which invariably brings smiles and positive evaluations (now, if that's not scientific—what is?), and brain imaging done at UCLA (not nearly as impressive a source, but I'll include it nonetheless). This second piece of research determined that social exclusion affects the brain in the same way as gut pain does. The brains of participants were scanned while they were excluded from social events, and subjects reported feeling social distress. The parts of the brain involved in emotional response to pain exhibited the same activity when a participant was rejected from group interaction as when physically hurt. "Social exclusion affects the brain in the same way as visceral pain does" (Arevalo, 2004). Include everyone in the action and you'll keep folks smiling.

Q: Is it better to mix folks up?

A: Oooooh, be careful here. If your purpose for the day is to increase articulation between departments or divisions that communicate poorly, or to generate new and novel thinking, then mix staff in carefully chosen groups. Assign groups with nametags on tables or team assignments made prior to or at session check-in. Never let people choose seats and then try to move them, as resentment and resistance follow. If mixing folks in a task or activity is useful for a short stint within the session, allow individuals to return to their own tables and friends once the task is complete. I can't tell you how often I get thanks for allowing this. Adults don't mind intermixing to work with new people occasionally, but highly resist being subjectively denied their own comfort spots. Give people choice whenever possible.

Prizes and Rewards

Q: If I use purposeful games to relax people, do you suggest prizes?

A: Prizes are great—for game rewards, for returning on time after lunch, or for any excuse you have for giving them. Here is the catch: ensure that tangible prizes are nonsense and virtually worthless. Folks will work as hard for trivial junk as they will for valuable rewards—but the latter brings serious competition, animosity, and resentment ("Our presentation was just as good," "We finished 3 seconds earlier, I'm sure"). *Avoid* tangible prizes with real value, unless everyone gets the prize. Then, it's positive and appreciated by all.

Q: Is it okay for a prize or a surprise to be totally unrelated to your purpose?

A: If a prize has some relevance, perhaps as a pun related to content or a joke regarding application, it's better: like a simple piece of yarn to wrap around your finger billed as a fabulous prize "to help you remember the key point of the day." Yet it's fine to be just goofy, too, and okay as well to build a little irrelevant surprise into a day. Perhaps do some spiffy trick that can't possibly be figured out and promise to reveal its secret at session end. Suspense builds, curiosity piques—and revelation becomes a sort of reward, with laughs, for sticking around.

Meaningful Mixers

Q: My opening mixers don't always yield positive results. Any suggestions to make them effective?

A: Choose mixers and openers both positive and appropriate to the audience. Avoid trite tasks that offend busy people, and always match activities to session goals. If the goal is to teach an innovative process, engage folks in an activity that imparts a surprising new skill—then debrief or make comments that segue into the session theme ("The impossible is no longer impossible when . . ."). Don't spend inordinate amounts of time on mixers, either. Nothing is more aggravating than using 20 minutes on a "funsy" task with professionals who prefer skipping the whole segment to do real work back at the office. I like tasks that last 1–3 minutes, maybe up to 5. No more, except in unusual circumstances in which the role of a mixer is more than setting a positive tone and direction for the day—it is actually a training task.

Figure 7.2

Mixer . . .

People Shuffle: Sets a light tone for a training. It also makes folks aware of how many similarities—or differences—they have with one another (even when they *think* they know each other well!). This also helps reluctant participants interact with others to prepare for regrouping.

Ask participants to stand in a large circle around the presenting room. Position yourself at the head of the circle to give directions:

> "We're going to "sort" ourselves into groups with people who share characteristics common to our own. I'll give you a category, and it will be *your* job to find others who share the same feelings as you (here, you might give an example, i.e., favorite color . . . all those who favor red stand here, blue cluster there, etc.). Do you understand? (Look for nods.) We will use music as a signal to start and stop, so you will have to move quickly and efficiently to find your group. When you hear the music begin, form groups. When you hear the music end, stop dead in your tracks and wait for my instructions. Begin the music as soon as you say, "Sort yourselves according to":

> - Where you were born
> - Your favorite pig-out food
> - Your dream vacation

And so on.

(Do one category at a time, pausing after each to ID the common feature of each cluster of people. Laugh and share surprise before going on to the next category topic.)

This activity requires enough room for all attendees to move and cluster easily and quickly. But it is impossible for folks not to smile, laugh, and feel surprise at the categories they share with colleagues!

Time and Organization

Q: How important is allocation of time?

A: Very! Don't waste a participant's most valuable commodity— *time*. Honor it, always. People are busy. Period. Start the session promptly (no more than 4–5 minutes past the announced time, to catch the last-minute arrivals but not anger the on-timers). Resume following breaks and timed tasks *exactly* when you indicated you would. No exceptions. Not only will people respect your agenda, but they will also appreciate your respect of their schedules.

Q: I frequently get complaints about my rambling and disorganization. Good grief, I plan and follow an outline! What do you suggest?

A: Perception is reality. If the plan isn't spelled out for sequential thinkers, they may think it doesn't exist. And whether they're right or wrong, the end result is the same: they're honked off. Try this: do a visual overview of the session at the start. Provide a list of the day's benefits and provide also a sequenced agenda. Then follow it both in your delivery and in the order of handouts. Nowhere does sequence and thoroughness count more than in handouts, but be sure that those key points are clearly listed, perhaps even in outline form to facilitate note taking. When appropriate, provide templates and charts to fill in during lecture or group reflection, and set aside time to complete those at the end of presentation segments. Also to help the more sequential learner, give a brief tour of handbook materials early in training and refer to specific sections or resources as you present. I often go so far as to include thumbnails of essential slides and refer to the corresponding handout page when projecting them.

Q: So it is safer to gear toward the analytical person, because the global processor will be OK without special attention?

A: Deal globally *and* analytically to hit every style—agendas and handouts, big picture overview and visuals along with generalizations, debriefing, and application opportunities for the global thinker. A constructive approach to session content (discovery) works well when the volume of content is modest (you must determine that) or the session purpose is problem solving (not application). In the latter case, multiple solutions are not just possible, they are desirable.

Handling Difficult Audiences

Q: Angry audiences—what do I do?

A: First, know your audience (again, rely on any presession information from contact persons indicating concerns or receptivity of the seminar group). In addition, you assess your audience as you personally welcome and converse with participants prior to the session start. Introduce yourself to each and ask, "What do you hope to accomplish at the seminar? What are your primary concerns?" You'll learn a *lot*. Then gear your opening or tailor your examples to their needs. If there's an issue that could cast a pall over the success of the day (and may not even have anything to do with you or your topic), honor their concerns briefly with a nonjudgmental remark ("I recognize these are tough times in contract negotiations . . .").

Anything that you can do to personalize the session will help. Wear an arm band to show support for an ailing colleague, put up a cartoon joke that frames a concern in a lighthearted way to diffuse tension, or tell a story to demonstrate your understanding ("I know how I felt when . . ."). A presenter who connects with the audience and gains their trust (that is, you understand) has a shot at success. Caution: Don't take sides in a controversy and don't indicate disgust— just show recognition and respect for concerns, and the audience will view you as sympathetic.

Q: Occasionally, I walk into a hornet's nest with an audience. Not choosing to attend, they resent the time away from a heavy workload.

A: Many folks *are* genuinely stressed and overtaxed, believing they can ill afford time away from their desks. Mention their issue ("I sense frustration. There appears to be some stress out there.") or acknowledge job demands, with a guarantee that the seminar will make that job easier. The trick is to have them discover a personal benefit for attending. Recording responses to questions like, "What do you bring to this session that could enrich it for all?" or "What would you need this session to provide to make it worth your while to attend?" might tap participant interest.

Q: What if the entire group has an issue with me or a resistance to the training or topic I am presenting?

A: If the entire group is difficult, face them head on. "Some of you may not perceive this training as one that benefits you." Try a quick activity: use a blank chart(s) or projected transparency to record two categories of responses. Ask folks to identify negative results from missing this meeting as well as benefits from attending this meeting. Notice that the questions in both cases channel responses to highlight the advantages for being at the session—what dastardly things might happen if you miss, what good might come if you attend? Steer clear of questions that channel answers toward why attending is wrong or why missing might be of benefit. You may get derogatory comments such as, "reprimands from the boss" when you solicit negatives for missing, but at least folks will see that it behooves them, to some degree, to attend.

Q: Won't the extroverts begin a diatribe, wasting time?

A: Get *all* involved in a fast-paced interactive task. Invite each table or pair of participants to generate at least two ideas for each chart. Record the ideas, no matter how brutally honest they are, and invite laughter, resigned attitudes, serious reflection, or whatever to come out. Thank each contributor, and when each chart is filled to satisfaction (done quickly and off-handedly), make a summary statement that sheds positive light on the event (It may be that *not* attending angers your boss, so the benefit for attending is that you are viewed as cooperative and a team player in the organization!). There are *always* benefits for attending (not always the obvious ones or those promoted by management). It might be survival within the organization or contributions showcased or perceptions of cooperation. It also might be networking opportunities, chances for a break from the grinding routine, or a chance to leave work 30 minutes early. Let them offer items for each list and record them so that they can see that not attending reaps bigger problems (potentially) for them than attending (reluctantly). Set aside the charts, and begin the seminar.

Q: What if the issue isn't diffused? Does the presenter just plow into the session?

A: If there is a single gripe held by the entire group, allow the audience to let off steam before you begin your seminar. Record their worries or concerns succinctly on a chart or overhead *without commenting on them* in any way. Then, thank them for opening up and sharing their concerns. Set aside the list and go on with the presentation. Folks usually feel relieved to have their concerns acknowledged and will be far more likely to attend to the day's business. If there's still animosity, create a verbal contract: "I won't . . . if you won't. . . ."

Q: Once in a while, it isn't an audience that's a problem—it's a single person. It's so uncomfortable!

A: Single antagonists require special handling. First, try sidling next to them. If this doesn't help, find common ground if possible—but under no circumstances should you lose your cool. Welcome their careful listening or critical thinking. Then, go on. (If all else fails, call a break and ask the individual, in private, what offends them.)

Humility

Q: When I attend a conference, it's amazing that presenters who are less knowledgeable than me are much more successful in their training. How do I win an audience, if not with the breadth and depth of my knowledge?

A: It is not just your level of knowledge that makes you a successful presenter or trainer. I assume any trainer or presenter has a firm grip on content and skills, or he or she wouldn't be in the position of training. So content knowledge is not the defining difference between success and failure in presenting (I assume you know your stuff, because if you're exposed as a phony, you're sunk). First, remember to let the audience see you as vulnerable—let them see your personality, share your stories, tell your mistakes, accept your blunders, laugh at yourself, and know you are human. Second, rarely does an audience take to a know-it-all. Perceived perfection often brings out the worst, as people become competitive and want to knock Mr. Perfect down a peg or two. Don't ask me why, it's just human nature.

Q: Then you say my goose is cooked because I know too much?

A: Nope, audiences *want* presenters to succeed. If they see you are much like them—frailties, shortcomings, and all—they will root for your success and overlook your faux pas. If they think you are a pompous goose, they'll do you in.

Setting Yourself Apart

Q: Is it best to really display my emotions when dealing with emotional issues?

A: Although you want to be friendly, sincere, unassuming, and vulnerable, you *never* want to wear your heart on your sleeve. Avoid three things:

- Pouring out your heart
- Sharing too much personal information
- Having extensive personal social contact with attendees

Believable leaders are elevated in the eyes of others, with an air of the unknown separating them ever so slightly. If a presenter becomes too familiar, he or she becomes like a member of the backyard bunch. And we all know that you can't be a prophet in your own backyard! (As Mark Twain said, "Familiarity breeds contempt")

Q: How do I rev up my audience about topics I really believe in?

A: Audiences love energy. That doesn't mean you have to be a human dynamo, but enthusiasm, body language, and zest for your topic can't be replaced by any measure of organization or planning. Wow 'em with your zeal. (Be sure it's real, however—folks can spot a phony a mile off. I don't recommend, "Always be sincere, whether you mean it or not." It can get you in trouble.)

Q: Any suggestions about handling folks who are resistant to change, even if their current approach has failed?

A: People are pretty predictable in two ways: (1) they resist change and (2) they gravitate to whatever makes them feel good about themselves. Take advantage of both. Recognize publicly that their reluctance is normal and understandable. They are wise to be wary; you, like them, don't willingly spend the energy and angst that change requires—unless it pays off. Treat audience members with respect, as both worthy individuals and knowledgeable professionals who have seen "great ideas" come and go. If you present yourself as a conduit for information that is beneficial to the learner, you have a better chance to earn respect—and maybe awe—for the contribution of *your* knowledge.

Q: What if their old ways are just plain ineffective or weak. Isn't it my duty to tell them?

A:It is better to let them discover it. Even though you are a change agent, begin the process toward change by honoring accomplishments, progress, or contributions made while doing it the old way. Speak to a group about building on the best of what exists, not scolding folks for being in the wrong place, which puts them on the defensive. People don't argue with their own data and ideas. Ask, What would you like to see work better? Where do you see the weakest link in this process? Where could we take your successes and improve upon them? Opportunity for improvement should be given to reach *common* goals; reprimands for mistakes or hand wringing for past failures should not.

Q: Last week, there was an ugly situation in my session, when a participant kept arguing and trying to impress me with her knowledge. She acted as though she knew as much as or more than I did. It was so uncomfortable for me and even for other folks in the training.

A: Anyone working with adult audiences eventually encounters this problem. The antagonist probably views herself as an expert rivaling you in ability or knowledge and is challenging you to compete. There also may be anger that *your* expertise is valued and hers—which is very similar—has been overlooked. Accept that this person may be skilled and knowledgeable—although lacking in the couth department. Avoid acting offended or trying to impress and outdo the challenger. It adds to others' discomfort and might cause confrontation with the attendee. Instead, honor her expertise: welcome her insight, credit any on-target reasoning, or thank her if a reflection is sophisticated. If her skill *is* impressive, ask if you could tap into it throughout the training (perhaps to lead a small group, serve as a resource when questions are asked by others, or present a segment of the topic). Always invite and then grant the choice to opt in or out.

Q: Should I allow an antagonist to help?

A: If truly skilled, he will be flattered and perhaps help in the facilitation. If he's bluffing or simply angry and resentful, he'll clam up quicker than a shell at low tide and leave you alone. After all, he doesn't want to draw attention to his limitations—he wants to show off or back you down. If you're not intimidated and welcome his expertise, you come out smelling like a rose nine out of ten times. Never go on the defensive, and never set people up. Simply be magnanimous enough to let them showcase their knowledge or to back out gracefully, saving face.

Q: Is there any way to make clear that a know-it-all really doesn't know it all?

A: I've had good luck with giving a sophisticated pretest, ensuring that there are questions on it no attendee could know ahead of time. It indicates to participants that you are indeed knowledgeable (for at least this session) and there is information they do not yet know.

DO'S AND DON'TS

- **Do** honor time
- **Do** admit errors, and then humbly move on
- **Do** involve *everyone*
- **Do** play calming music when breaks begin
- **Do** use upbeat, fast-tempo music to recall folks back from break
- **Don't** forget adults love choices!
- **Don't** become too familiar with your audience—friendly yes, familiar no
- **Don't** use off-color jokes or stories
- **Don't** talk politics
- **Don't** lose your cool

CHAPTER EIGHT

That's a Wrap!

The caboose doesn't always have to be red.

Susan Jones

THE LASTING IMPRESSION

Once in a while, remembering the rules pays off. Case in point: a keynote speech for a prestigious audience, a number of years ago. I was pretty wet behind the ears in the keynoting department, but had painstakingly prepared the most organized, best visually supported, and practiced speech I could. Since all bases were covered, that speech was sure to go well. Famous last words.

About 10 minutes into the keynote, the audience was visibly agitated—shifting in their seats, eyes darting, whispers flying. My head was swirling, and panicked thoughts flooded my mind as my career seemed to be ending right there on that stage! Yet somewhere in the back of my mind came the words, "First and last, first and last!"

I gave a break . . . yep, gave them a 5-minute break in the midst of a short keynote. I said something like, "Looks like I'm having a clumsy start—take 5 minutes to stand and stretch your legs, and when you return I'll deliver to you the most important information of the day." People literally stared at me, stunned. They slowly rose and shuffled out confused and slightly entertained. And I figured not a one of them would return.

Now, my mind was grasping at straws to find a way to turn that speech around, to save myself, when that rule pushed into my thoughts. "First and last" means that an audience has a tendency to remember mainly the beginnings and endings (not middles) of a presentation. This was the test and, by golly, the old rule helped me pass.

Folks did come back—amazingly, on time. They trickled in with measured curiosity (I figure they wanted to witness the self-destruction of a novice). I began again—with a strong message, to a surprisingly rapt audience. And it ended—with a standing ovation. Wow. What a lesson.

The rule is that no matter what else, one must start and end *strongly* if a presentation is to succeed. Strong starts set the stage for positive expectations; strong endings stick as the last impression. They make or break a presentation. What did I do during the break on that day? I scrambled off that stage and wedged between seats to get to three middle-aged women who remained in the auditorium. "Ladies," I said. "What do you *want* from this day?" They told me—oh, they sure did. They wanted bottom lines. Not to be talked *to,* but talked *with.* Not inundated with a prepared text, but treated to practicality. "What difference does all this research make on how kids learn?" Time was short, their statements were matter-of-fact, and I listened. *Listened.*

And I changed. I abandoned my structured plans, my detailed notes, and my beautifully sequenced visuals. Gears were shifted, folks. No more podium—I stood at the edge of the stage and looked out into my audience members' eyes. I paused and began anew, speaking with them, each and every one, by answering concerns of my three ladies, earnestly and honestly. I felt my energy rise, let my body communicate, and I had 'em—in the palm of my hand.

Certainly not every impending disaster ends so successfully. But experience really is the best teacher, and I never again took lightly the importance of a strong finish. It correlates with success.

QUESTIONS AND ANSWERS

The Three Features of a Quality Closer

Q: So endings primarily serve to establish a lasting emotional impression?

A: Any good closing accomplishes three things: (1) it guarantees that the audience is aware of personal gains from the session;

(2) reinforces, reviews, or demands application of the theme, lesson, or content of the session; and (3) provides a lasting, positive emotional message that the listener takes away. Often, all three are accomplished in a single activity. Yet whether your ending is stair stepped with sequenced mini-events or a leap to dramatic finale, be sure that none of the desirable accomplishments of a closing are ignored. And whatever else, focus on item 3. Without it, not much else counts. I repeat: "If the audience ain't happy, ain't nobody happy."

Audience Awareness of Session Gains

Q: Why awareness? Is it really necessary to point out session gains?

A: Adults don't always consciously tally gains, and lackadaisical tracking can be reflected in negative evaluations. Even if it's not an accurate picture of your training thoroughness, that old "perception is reality" will get you every time. For instance, I received negative feedback from a daylong session years back, expressing dissatisfaction over the number of tips and strategies promised in the session versus the number delivered. That feedback, accurate or not, reflected my ineffectiveness. It wasn't enough that I had actually delivered more than promised, I had to convince the listener. I needed to build awareness of session value and gains.

Q: Okay, so how do you do that without getting defensive with the audience?

A: It can be as simple as promising a defined number of ideas and then counting them—both verbally and visually—by recording them on charts, overheads, or slides as they are revealed and discussed. The overview of a session goal might include "Identify and discuss five methods of. . . ." Then as content is delivered, methodically draw attention to the fulfillment of the promise. "Remember those five methods? Well, here is number 1!" Tell them. Then be sure they heard you tell them. Then make them tell what they heard.

Q: Is this enough? What if I don't have "five" of this, "two" of that? I work with many facts, much logic and reasoning, and practical application.

A: There are several suggestions. First, throughout your training, build in short (1–2 minute) opportunities to reflect on what has been heard and to jot down anything significant in a session journal. Near day's end, build in a 3–5 minute activity for participants to check notes, charts, or journals with a colleague. Have them checked for accuracy, thoroughness or omissions.

Another activity, 8-Ball, is quicker and more interactive— actually tallying gains and doubling as an embedded review or summarizing task. Here, each participant is asked to record four significant ideas, applications, or suggestions from the training. As always, time the task and when time expires, direct them to borrow two new ideas from the lists of other colleagues, to reach a total of six. Keep going until each person holds a card with eight new pieces of valuable information gleaned from the session. (And there's a bonus: folks are forced to revisit their notes!)

Q: Good grief, at the end of a session it is often a race with the clock. What if I don't have time for movement and group interaction?

A: Create a speedy list of new ideas as a whole group activity. Ask folks to work with colleagues seated near them to generate between two and five new ideas from the day. Provide 30–45 seconds of work time, and then invite small groups to share—by calling out—their ideas as you rapidly list them on a chart or overhead. Challenge the audience to name five—and then build to between ten and twenty-five total or to hit thirty-two (to win some grandiose (trivial) prize)! They will gleefully search their notes, rack their brains, and spin new ideas to rise to the challenge. Recording these ideas on a chart or overhead, quickly and casually, astounds the audience with the quantity of information they've received. There is no arguing about the wealth of the day when participants generate the bounty themselves. Evaluations improve, guar-an-teed.

Review, Rehearsal, and Application

Q: How about the application piece? Is it essential that folks end with reflection on ways to apply new learning?

A: In a keynote, the purpose might be to entertain or to change audience thinking or perspective. Application, therefore, is not an automatic next step. If you are facilitating or training, on the other hand, you bet

Figure 8.1

Review

Sequenced Circle Review: This energizing task combines movement and a brief review of material. It is effective at the end of a training segment or the entire training! It is effective with groups of 4 or more people (The greater the number working together, the more challenging). Adequate room for movement is necessary.

Prepare as many slips as you have members for each group. On each slip, a question and an answer will appear—but not a matched set. Separate and mix up the slips, and place one set per envelope, one envelope for each group. The goal is for folks to dump out the slips, disperse one to each group member, and race to be the first group to arrange themselves in the correct circular order to reflect a correct question and answer sequence.

I have: a presenter with a measure of vulnerability **Start Here** *Who has:* The largest group size for which to use charts as a primary communication device?	*I have:* 30 *Who has:* The ideal size for small-group interactions?
I have: 2–4 *Who has:* How long a presenter should circulate with participants before a session even begins?	*I have:* 15–20 *Who has:* The % a presenter's words have the overall impact on an audience?
I have: content *Who has:* The maximum number of minutes as audience should engage in monotonous tasks before inserting an energizer?	*I have:* determining when participats need a break *Who has:* What handouts should mirror?
I have: 7 *Who has:* What the 1–2–3 rule deals with?	*I have:* 15 minutes *Who has:* What helps build audience rapport?

application is necessary. In fact, real learning requires change in behavior, and that doesn't happen unless knowledge and skill are connected to the context of each person's life. Make sure the final task, whether done individually or in small groups, includes conversation or products that demonstrate application of course content.

Q: Back to the activity approach. I love the interaction—any other ways I can build a sort of game atmosphere into review?

A: Here's a sure-fire suggestion. Decide on two to five session categories or questions for review. Write one category or question per card, using as many individual cards as there are participants. Distribute one to each person, and ask for reflection on the meaning or significance of each person's assigned category. Then instruct participants to record their thoughts on the card. Provide approximately 1 minute to work, before directing people to trade cards with a colleague and begin the process again, with each individual asked to

- Reflect on the newest category or question
- Read ideas already recorded by others
- Add their thoughts to the card

The exchange and recording process is repeated twice more, with the last trade stopping after reading the ideas recorded by others. Request that participants reflect on all these ideas and identify the one that is most significant or meaningful.

These most significant ideas are then shared with the facilitator, who records them for subsequent discussion. The entire group, or small groups reconvened, can peruse and critique lists, adding to or correcting them as they do. Notice, this is anonymous and thus safe, interactive, and enjoyable. Plus, it forces review!

Q: I like the idea of tallying for review, but don't always want group activities. Give me something fun for individuals.

A: Find things for each person to accumulate each time a new bit of course content is learned. Accumulation results in a grand prize: to win, the items earned must reach some predetermined total, or construct some product, or solve some mystery. Ways to tally:

- Provide each person with a zip-seal baggie containing jigsaw puzzle pieces. Participants earn one puzzle piece for each new idea gained. As pieces are earned throughout training, the puzzle is assembled until the whole is revealed. A completed puzzle might contain a message that reinforces the theme ("A team that cooperates is a team that wins!"). Anyone who deciphers the message before session end wins a prize.
- Provide each table with one large bowl of interlocking shapes. Participants earn links and adjoin them as they are obtained. When the chain reaches a predetermined length (perhaps it crosses the table or extends from elbow to wrist), a prize is won.
- Participants work to acquire enough tiny marshmallows to fill a cup or foam squares to fill in a grid.

Adults seek new ideas in order to win pieces—and the prize. Note these can be team as well as individual projects, to encourage conversation, interaction, and interdependence.

Q: I prefer an ongoing, individual count woven seamlessly into a day's activity, rather than setting aside formal time to reflect and record. Would I explain the process early in the training, so folks begin immediately to tally?

A: Yes, indeed, right up front. Here's an easy individual tally task: Post and point out a bull's-eye chart early in the session.

Figure 8.2

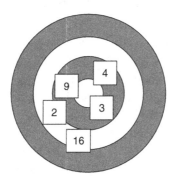

Provide small sticky notes on each table, making available one per participant. Say, "Record the number of *new* ideas you would need to make this session worth the time and effort it takes to attend it." Pause while they record their number. Once done, ask folks to keep track of new ideas, and when (if) they hit their target, to post the note on the bull's-eye.

Q: Is it reasonable to require a written plan for implementation of course content before participants depart a session?

A: Certainly, assuming there is ample time in the session for the training, reflection, and production of such a plan. Provide specific directions for formal reflection: "Identify the most important ideas from this seminar. How will your work be impacted by them?" Circulate and comment as individuals respond, providing feedback as they work. Remember, unless this is a for-credit class that requires grades, your purpose for feedback is diagnostic, to help gauge and guide participant growth.

If there aren't at least 15–30 minutes available within the session to finish an application project, request the project be completed or submitted postsession. Regardless of format and timetable for completion, provide personalized feedback regarding the project. Comment via e-mail, accompany returned projects with correspondence, or arrange site visits to observe application and debrief.

Q: Give me an example of an ending application task that won't result in attendees staring at me blankly for direction.

A: Narrow the question, and provide guidance. Say perhaps, "Think of the most personally difficult aspect of working with adult audiences. Write a goal based on the improvement you hope to make. Use ideas and procedures highlighted in this training, and incorporate them into a personal improvement plan."

Provide a project exemplar, modeling the process necessary to complete it. ("My problem is . . . [audience hostility], my goal is . . . [to deal effectively with negative detractors], and the strategy I will use is . . .). Remember, give the big picture first and details are filled in later.

Q: My problem is not in wording a question or assigning an application product, but rather ensuring all attendees get the big picture.

A: For this, I would do solo brainstorming (see Chapter 5) followed by small group brainstorming of the same question. At session end, or the end of a training segment, ask individuals to reflect on questions such as these:

- Summarize the key concepts of this training.
- Identify gaps that still exist in your knowledge.
- What do you still need to know about the topic?
- How will you translate this training into professional practice?
- Identify barriers to applying new information.

Ask attendees to join their small or table groups to discuss their answers. Peruse responses from small group brainstorming, and then with the entire group identify concerns or discuss ways to overcome obstacles. This invites content application, interaction, and problem solving while answering individual concerns. Time? At least 30 to 45 minutes.

Positive Endings

Q: I use quotes and stories to wrap up a session on a positive note. Is this a weak way to end?

A: Nope. You could have a winner, but *make sure the message fits the session theme.* I have listened to many great ending quotes—but sometimes not for the speech I attended. Disjointed endings leave one kinda cold (Where the heck did that come from?). Assuming a selected quote or story has a theme befitting the presentation message, I have found quoting an author with particular audience appeal *doubles* the impact. Talking with history teachers? Quote Teddy Roosevelt. With business retailers? Find words from Sam Walton. You get the picture—one more connection, one more way to honor the audience. And for maximum effect, reveal the author's identity *after* the quote sinks in.

Q: How about humor? Always, sometimes, or never appropriate for an ending?

A: If it fits the theme of your message and tone of the presentation, then yes. But be sure your humor is really funny or clever. Remember, nothing off color or demeaning or you'll end on a downer, which is the direction your evaluation ratings will go. Short, quick jokes with clear punch lines or short, clever stories with strong messages. Incidentally, people *love* stories—in any form—and absolutely love to laugh. Following up a lighthearted story or a winner of a joke with upbeat, fast-tempo music puts folks in a great mood for filling out evaluation forms, too.

Q: Is it possible to kill two birds with one stone by combining review of material with positive emotion? Or are shortcuts shortchanges to the audience?

A: Efficiency is what you describe. If you can snag a single task that serves multiple purposes, you don't want to lose that fish. Here's one that is game-like, quick, interactive, full of mystique, demands review of material, and makes folks move. It's the Three Card Toss, a trick I learned from a master trainer, Dave Arch, from Creative Training in Minneapolis, Minnesota. Have folks tear paper into three small pieces, approximately 2 inches by 2 inches. Here are the rules:

1. Number the pieces, 1, 2, and 3.

2. On card #1, write something you heard today that validates you as a (manager?)

3. On card #2, jot down an action you have taken in the past and now realize was a mistake—you'll never do it again!

4. On card #3, write down the single best idea you heard today.

Then, instruct each person to arrange the papers in front of themselves, horizontally, in any order (1,2,3 or 3,1,2, etc.). Give the following instructions:

- Put your hand on paper #1 and exchange it with the card to its right (if there is no card to the right, leave it where it is).
- Pick up card #2 and exchange it with the card to its left (again, if there is no card to the left, leave it alone).
- Pick up card #3 and exchange it with the card to its right, if indeed there is a card to its right. Otherwise, leave it alone.
- Next, pass your hand over all three cards.
- Instruct participants to pick up the center card and place it in a safe spot, as it is important.

- Then, have them again pass a hand over the remaining two cards. Lifting the card farthest to the right, have them place it next to their heart, because it will make tremendous difference for future success.
- Then, have people pick up the remaining card (which is always card #2) and tear, scrunch, and discard it—never to be a part of anything you do again.

They will be mystified and delighted—a great way to end!

Figure 8.3

Close With a Bang!

Closers sometimes serve as celebration. If neither review nor profundity is essential, go for "fun" by offering a "contest" with prizes! Of course, the trick is rigged so no fabulous (er, valuable) prizes can be won . . . but the silly, goofy ones can be!

Prepare 3 business-sized "trick" envelopes ahead of time. In each, place one folded paper listing a silly prize tucked in, under, and behind the sealing flap.

Also place inside the envelope, but *outside* and over the flap, a second folded sheet of paper with a fabulous, desirable prize.

Before the contest, announce that the audience has been so super that you want to afford them a chance to win a wonderful prize. Show them the 3 envelopes, numbered 1, 2, or 3, each containing a "wonderful" prize. Of course, funding constraints dictate that only one prize can be awarded—but with the help of participants, 2 of the envelopes will be eliminated, leaving one last, winning envelope which contains a prize awarded to every attendee.

*You, the presenter, *must* be the only one who handles the envelopes.

Walk up to any audience member, and fan out all three envelopes. Ask them to tap the one envelope they wish to *eliminate* from the contest, then hold the envelopes as they make their choice. Take the tapped envelope and open it, removing the "fabulous" prize tucked over the flap (an all-expense paid trip to Rome?). Hand the sheet to the 'tapper' to read aloud to the whole group, and groan with them in agony over losing that prize. Continue the exact same process with the last two envelopes, until only one final envelope remains.

Then announce, "We now have one last envelope. It is the one that contains the prize that each of you will win!" Create a fanfare, with gestures and drama, to build suspense as you remove the prize—only this time, remove the prize sheet lying *under* the flap (the crummy one!) while the fabulous one hidden in the envelope remains untouched. Hand the crummy prize sheet to the third participant to read to the entire audience, revealing the prize that "each and every one" of them is lucky enough to win! (Now you'll really hear groans!)

Figure 8.4

Color Disk Review: Movement, reflection, and recall combine to create a quality collaborative review. In advance of the end of the session, tape up a variety of large colorful disks around the training room (approximately one different color disk per 6-7 participants is ideal). On the back side, tape a word, phrase, or question that is representative of key concepts or topics from the training. Each group becomes responsible for their unique concept.

Ask participants to view the disks taped around the perimeter of the room, and stand beside the color disk of their choice. Warn them, however, that no group can contain more than 6 (or 7, etc.) people, so if the group they join is already filled to capacity, they must go on and join another color disk team.

Next, ask the group to lift the disk and read the back term. Provide the group 3–5 minutes to generate answers to share afterward with the entire group. You might require each group to choose a recorder and spokesperson to increase reporting efficiency. When the groups report, the trainer might capture ideas on an overhead, or might ask, "anything missing?" from the remainder of the participants before moving on to the next group report.

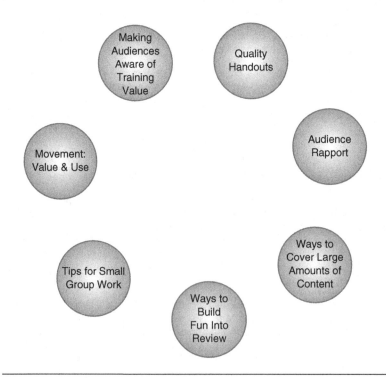

Q: Emotion? Sure. And I understand ending strongly. But even when I end with a positive story or anecdote, some folks gather up items and leave before I finish!

A: It's generally the final 2–3 minutes when such departures occur. So *always end on time.* They'll love you if you end 5 minutes early and loathe you if you end 5 minutes late. The way I figure, the cost of a 5-minute overrun is too high to chance disaster. Forgo even the strongest planned ending if it means you will go overtime more than 1 minute. In those cases, substitute a short, one- or two-sentence backup finisher for any presentation you do, just for times like this. Again, I repeat: *end on time.* (Maybe then there'll be time for a standing ovation!)

Q: Any rituals for the end of a session—things you always do, no matter what?

A: If it's humanly possible, stand near the exit door and thank folks for attending, contributing, or volunteering—even those who were a thorn in your side. Best darned lasting impression you'll ever make. And unless that extra 3 minutes makes you miss your plane, there is no better way to spend it.

DO'S AND DON'TS

- **Do** help participants tally their gains so they are aware of the value of your seminar!
- **Do** find ways to force review and application of content
- **Do** be certain stories and jokes reinforce your message
- **Do** remain positive to the end
- **Do** end on time!
- **Do** bid people farewell as they exit
- **Don't** spend all your time on the middle—it is the beginning and ending of your session that makes or breaks you. It's what your participants will remember
- **Don't** end on a downer—finish on a positive, hopeful note

CHAPTER NINE

Evaluations

Make It the Best Plant Possible and Then Keep Weeding, Watering, and Talking to It Sweet

We grow because we struggle, we learn and overcome.

R. C. Allen

S o much heart and soul goes into presenting and facilitating. The road to excellence in this vocation is long and bumpy, and traveling it takes time, toil, and a measure of courage. Sound like a humbling journey? It can be.

CONSISTENCY: AN ELUSIVE TARGET

No matter the experience or prestige off the platform, speaking before a group is a great leveler. There's no hiding from folks; they walk right into your mind and enter your thoughts. And they judge you—immediately and throughout your delivery—and reflect those feelings with formal evaluations of your effectiveness. There are tangibles and intangibles that affect such assessments, going well beyond quality of message: different audiences, different venues, different contexts, different moods, different foci, different conditions, different days. And the endless combination of variables makes consistent excellence tough to achieve. The quality of work stutters, so on any given day even the most highly skilled people perform *on average* anywhere from fair to best. Improvement comes from raising the *average*—not from hitting an occasional home run. In that regard, a professional communicator is like a baseball player, as a solid batting average is more important than a few memorable hits. What counts is the consistency of hits; it's the performance average that earns the ranking. Keep the bar high, clear it ever more convincingly, and positive assessments will come rolling in. Routinely. *Consistently.*

Before we dive into assessments, I'd like to preface with seven important items woven throughout this book that are real Secrets to Success. Take care of these first, and then fine tune.

Checklist for Winning Them Over: The Top Seven Secrets for Success[1]

√ Let your personality show. Be real.
√ Never work to impress anyone. Work to *give* to everyone.
√ Recognize and credit the work of others. Often.
√ Showcase knowledge with personal stories and struggles, not with your resumé (no one likes a braggart).
√ Invite and welcome *participants'* ideas; value *their* examples.
√ Prove that *your* message makes *their* life easier.
√ Let people *enjoy* themselves.

Now, let's get specific.

INVITING IMPROVEMENT

A couple of tips. First, be sure you are evaluated each time you present. That means informal self-evaluation, but it also means formal evaluations such as participant feedback and observer critiques. Look for trends, recurring comments, and repeating themes. And don't overlook positive comments! They're just as important as negative ones, as they indicate what you should *continue* to do. Remember, growth and improvement build upon existing strengths—don't throw out everything to start from scratch each time you tackle a new challenge.

Next, lose the thin skin. Toughen up and look at yourself objectively, not defensively. A quote by Norman Vincent Peale captures it: "The trouble with most of us is that we would rather be ruined by praise than saved by criticism" (Blaydes, 2003, p. 114). That doesn't mean that every negative comment warrants our attention. The best speech of all time can be given, and I guarantee someone in the audience will think it stinks. They might've had an argument with their boss, or they feel lousy, or they just don't like the presenter's looks. Toughen up and ignore those anomalies—a formal evaluation or two that are contrary to the trend of the remainder should get little notice.

I have even asked trusted colleagues to sort through and remove stand-alone negative feedback before I scour evaluations. Why? So I don't dwell on the nitpickers.

I learned that after my presentation to a group of 125 folks on a hot day in a facility with no air-conditioning. I worked myself silly to provide a high-quality session and felt darned good about it. Until I read the evaluations. Oh, they were good—but for one that ripped me up one side and down the other because I had "disgusting, dry elbows!" Now, I didn't need to read that and it haunted me for days, silly as that sounds. (But I'll tell you, I never forget to put lotion on my elbows, even if I'm wearing a long sleeve jacket). Nooo, no thin skin *here.*

On the other hand, if the stack of negatives is more than 5% of the total, I might wince, but I read every single negative comment. Because such a percentage indicates *I have a problem,* and by golly there'll be some fine-tuning. A mention of the same issue on several evaluations is a serious concern. No excuses. Now, let's grow.

QUESTIONS AND ANSWERS

Informal Feedback

Q: This informal feedback. What do you mean?

A: Read your audience continually and adjust immediately. Do a running evaluation as to how you are handling the session. Look at your audience and respond to them.

Q: What criteria should I use to self-evaluate as I deliver a session?

A: Look for these:

1. Attention and engagement: Are folks making eye contact with you, moving their eyes, and shifting their bodies to follow you physically?

2. Facial expressions and body language: Do you get nods, occasional smiles, and expected reactions to your actions or rolled eyes, defensive posture, and slow reactions to requests?

3. Clarity of understanding and productivity: Do folks work earnestly to accomplish what you ask, without resistance? Does the audience appear to be following you? Is there confusion or misunderstanding of expectations?

Q: Any other ways to tell, in the midst of a session, whether you are on target? Some of my audiences appear content and satisfied, until I get the formal evaluations and learn otherwise. I have no opportunity to adjust within the presentation and correct things.

A: Force the issue. If the person who hired you is in attendance, ask them at a break or at lunch whether you are meeting their expectations. If not, make adjustments on the spot. For attendee feedback, use a progress board to invite session participants to give anonymous feedback using sticky notes placed on the board at break, lunch, and so on. Ask them to indicate whether you are hitting the target. A variation is to provide anonymous "Still Need" sheets that are turned in at a break halfway through a session to provide a safe means of feedback from attendees. This leaves ample time to address participant concerns.

Formal Feedback

> *If you really want to see yourself, borrow somebody else's eyes.*
>
> Susan Jones

Q: Sometimes formal evaluations criticize things I can't control—should I pay attention?

A: Set guidelines for what you take to heart—what to acknowledge—so the audience credits your concern for their comfort. Criticism of the facility (unless you own and run it yourself) should be passed on to management. Yet if there is a criticism of something you *can* change, and if such change improves your presentation, then *change.* For every one person who openly comments on an issue, you can be certain there are others who feel the same way but keep silent. Clothes too distracting? Tone 'em down. Voice too high pitched? Work to lower it. Sat too long? Provide more changes of state. But dry elbows? Give me a break.

Q: Negative evaluations devastate me. But shouldn't I be strong enough to read every comment if I really want to grow?

A: Don't expect perfection from yourself. Even seasoned masters react strongly to negative comments—it really nettles them. Presenters are sensitive to audiences and give inordinate amounts of attention to feedback received. The bottom line is we do need some strokes—*positive* comments—to bolster us for our next training. If you expose yourself routinely to the unfair or petty comments, it erodes self-confidence and can interrupt the self-assured flow needed for great communication. Read and adjust to all thoughtful or constructive criticism (even if it is blunt or unforgiving), but sort out the chaff from the wheat. Stack the deck for self-preservation.

Q: What do you do with this "thoughtful" criticism?

A: Debrief your own session. Mark what you did and did not complete on your session agenda and place it in the event file. Note carefully what went well and what needs improvement. Keep a written list of considerations to which you can refer when preparing for the next training—and then, work to raise that bar.

Q: Should participants routinely provide formal evaluation of the presenter?

A: Yes, except in the case of keynote speeches. If a hiring client doesn't provide an assessment form, provide one yourself. It's the best way to get sound information for professional growth and improvement. Plus, copies of positive evaluations can come in handy for references later on.

Q: How do you get information that is detailed enough to direct personal improvement? People often skip filling in comment sections or they write useless generalities.

A: Carefully construct evaluations that prompt feedback information specifically of interest to you. Evaluations that request number rankings only, as on a Likert scale, don't provide the detail needed to indicate why something was good or bad. Similarly, a section that just requests comments gives the evaluator no guidelines for providing *helpful* information to the presenter and is often left blank or is full of extraneous detail unimportant to the purpose of the session (*Why weren't there any cherry Danish?*). Ask pointed questions:

- What part of this training is most useful to you?
- What would you *not* change about this presentation?
- What more do you need?
- How can you use the skills and information from today?
- What are the next steps?
- What could you recommend to make this an even stronger session?

Q: How does this type of questioning help?

A: Answers to those questions provide insight into how you functioned as a vehicle for reaching your goal: *your effectiveness*. It solicits constructive feedback as evaluators identify what worked and what did not. Scales and number rankings don't say much, except "you're good" or "you're bad." That's a snapshot judgment, not a tool for improvement.

Q: It seems like some people feel they must criticize something. How do I keep people positive, instead of negative?

A: It's all in the questioning. Don't ask, "What's wrong," ask "What's strong" or how to make things better.

Collegial Feedback

Q: What if a written evaluation doesn't reconcile with my observations or participant comments made during the session? I've occasionally been shocked at negative evaluations that contradict my own feelings about how a session went. How can I figure out what went wrong?

A: Remember the participant who complained that not enough tips had been given during training? I was incensed that anyone would criticize me on that point, as I prided myself in giving out gobs of ideas. Saying I didn't provide strategies was rather like saying a centipede needed more legs (at least that's how I felt). So the next time I gave the training, I chose a trusted professional to sit in the audience. Ah! Better than eyes on the back of my head, she could be my observer. I asked the friend to tally the techniques I shared and to observe the session to give me her take on the day. By the way, I promised twenty tips for the session and my observer stopped counting at seventy-three! I learned much that day.

Q: Is a professional observer just there to prove or disprove attendees' opinions? Is this about ego?

A: No, no. Remember, success is measured by one's *effectiveness*. Whether or not I provided ample content was not the point. The fact that the attendee believed I failed is what mattered. I had been ineffective for that person. The question, then, was why? I had stumbled on a most valuable vehicle for improvement: a collegial evaluation—not one read by supervisors, handed to an employer, or quantifiable for formal reports. Its purpose instead is to experience our own presentation through the eyes—and ears—of a professional we trust.

Q: How did you begin this?

A: I stumbled on this process a number of years ago, quite by accident. Christine Tomasino, a highly respected, bright colleague, spontaneously and informally debriefed me after attending one of my sessions. Spewing compliments, she wanted me to know where I had really clicked. I appreciated her input, but discovered that it was not her compliments that I hung on. It was her suggestions and recommendations for improvement. I was mesmerized by real, honest feedback. "Was there anything that was flat?" I asked. And that began the process.

Q: So how do you choose this professional observer?

A: An observer must be someone whom we respect professionally, who is knowledgeable about presenting and keen on nonverbal language. Oh, and one more thing. They must be brutally honest when a notepad and checklist are placed in their hands (brutal honesty is different from having a mean streak or a personal agenda, by the way).

To do this requires a skilled and honest colleague who's available once or twice a year and a genuine desire on *your* part to grow and improve. You can't be looking for syrupy compliments (although a few of those don't hurt, when well deserved), and you can't be argumentative about the observations.

Q: Why do I need a colleague to observe?
I use quality written evaluations from attendees
to provide feedback.

A: If one's improvement depends solely on participant evaluation ratings, resulting change will be driven by incomplete data. Any change must be made for only one reason—to reach the session goal: driving home a theme, teaching concepts or skills, imparting a message. We presenters aren't of primary importance: *our purpose in presenting is*. And any evaluation of us must deal with our success, or lack thereof, in communicating a message. The key word is *effectiveness*. Participant evaluations might indicate we fell short, but rarely provide insights as to why.

Q: What kinds of things are important for a
collegial observer to note?

A: The observer is not focused on you, the presenter, but on the audience and its *re*action to every *action* you take. It's your impact that's being measured, your effectiveness that's being gauged. What works and what does not. These are the types of questions you want answered:

- How do I function as a vehicle for reaching my goal?
- At what exact point did I start to lose the audience? Was it my voice? My expression? My body language? My words? The choice or structure of an activity?
- When did they tune me out—or engage and tune in?
- How did participants function in the time allocated for the task? What was their reaction when time expired?
- What positively impacted the audience?

- Where did the message get muddled?
- When, how, or why (at what point) did the audience arrive at understanding?
- What brought laughter and smiles?
- When and in response to what did participants shoot glances of disgust?
- What caused people to yawn?
- When did the hair go up on the back of their necks?
- When did folks begin to shuffle feet and shift in chairs?
- When were they leaning forward, in anticipation of the next task?

Observing that type of information is tough to do solo, no matter how skilled you are in reading people. And it sure doesn't come from reading comments on formal evaluations.

Do's and Don'ts

- **Do** debrief your own session, noting what went well and what needs to change
- **Do** self-assess continually during presentations
- **Do** ask evaluation questions that yield answers rich in information
- **Do** focus on your effectiveness
- **Don't** become defensive—become better
- **Don't** solicit negative comments on formal evaluations
- **Don't** rely solely on number rankings for evaluation of presenter effectiveness

and . . .

- **Don't** forget to put lotion on your elbows

We are what we repeatedly do. Excellence, then, is not an act, but a habit.

Aristotle, 384–322 BCE

Note

1. For additional "Secrets for Success," see Susan Jones' Web site: www.susanjjones.com

References

Arevalo, J. D. (2004). The pain of isolation. *Staff Developer Update*, 6(1). Retrieved January 14, 2004, from www.thebrainstore.com (Article is currently unavailable from the Web site)

Barth, R. (1990). Retrieved July 6, 2004, from the Eisenhower National Clearinghouse Web site: www.enc.org/professional/learn/change/resources/readings/document.shtm?input=ACQ-137035–7035

Bartlett, J. (1982). The teaching for Merikare. In (R. O. Faulkner, trans.), *Familiar quotations* (p. 4, para. 8). Boston: Little, Brown.

Blaydes, J. (2003). *The educator's book of quotes*. Thousand Oaks, CA: Corwin Press.

Bower, B. (2003). Gestures help words become memorable. *Science News*, 163(16).

Brainy Quote. (2004). Mark Twain. (1835–1920). Retrieved June 8, 2004, from www.brainyquote.com/quotes/authors/m/mark_twain.html.

Brink, S. (2000, October 16). Sleepless society. *U.S. News and World Report*, pp. 63–72.

Carper, J. (2000). *Your miracle brain*. New York: Harper Collins.

Cortright, R. N., Collins, H. L., Rodenbaugh, D. W., & DiCarlo, S. E. (2003). Student retention of course content is improved by collaborative-group testing. *Advances in Physiology Education*, 27(3), 102–108.

Fahey, J. A. (2000). Water, water everywhere. *Educational Leadership*, 53(8), 33–37.

Gutin, J. C. (2000, January). Quotable quotes. *Readers Digest,* p. 65.

Marzano, R. J., Pickering, D. J., & Pollock, J. E. (2001). *Classroom instruction that works*. Alexandria, VA: Association for Supervision and Curriculum Development.

Peoples, D. (1992). *Presentation plus*. New York: Wiley.

Pike, R. W. (1994). *Creative training techniques handbook*. Minneapolis, MN: Lakewood Books.

Quotation Center. (2004). Gardner, Herbert. Retrieved May 11, 2004, from www.cyber-nation.com/victory/quotation/subjects/quotes_speakers andspeaking.html

Selsor, K. (2003). Intrinsic motivation = increased learning. *Staff Developer Update, 5*(11). Retrieved November 16, 2003, from www.thebrain storenews.com (Article is currently unavailable from the Web site)

Smith, S. M., Ward, T. B., & Schumacher, J. S. (1993). Constraining effects of examples in a creative generation task. *Memory and Cognition, 21,* 837–845.

Wolfe, P., Burkman, M. A., & Streng, K. (2000). The science of nutrition. *Educational Leadership, 57*(6), 54–59.

World of Quotes. (2004). R. C. Allen. Retrieved July 6, 2004, from www .worldofquotes.com/author/R.-C.-Allen/1/index.html

Index

Acceptance, gaining, 26, 51
  See also Audience acceptance
Active participation, ensuring (Q&A),
  49–50
  See also Presenter technique;
    Reviews
Agendas and overheads (Q&A),
  31–32
Analogies, effectiveness of, 43–44
Analytical participants, 82–83
Angry audiences, handling. *See*
  Difficult audiences, handling
  (Q&A)
Answers, when you don't have the
  (Q&A), 75
Antagonists, handling, 85, 87–88
Appeal factors, 72
Appearance, for success, 11
Application, review, and rehearsal
  (Q&A), 92–97, 93*f,* 95*f*
Aristotle, 110
Arrival preparation. *See* Facility setup
Articles, background, 7
Ash, M. K., 42
Assessment forms, 106–107
  See also Evaluations
Attention, directing (Q&A), 69
Attention, regaining (Q&A), 49
  See also Presenter technique
Attention and sleep, 10
Audience, monitoring an, 55–57
Audience acceptance
  acknowledging knowledge and
    know-how, 28

agendas and overviews (Q&A),
  31–32
building audience rapport, 27–28
changing audience's point of view
  (Q&A), 30–31
do's and don'ts, 35–36
gaining acceptance, 26
honoring audience expertise
  (Q&A), 29–30
increasing visibility (Q&A), 30
introductions and openers (Q&A),
  32–34, 33*f*
positive communication (Q&A),
  34–35
working around personal quirks,
  28–29
Audience awareness, of session gains
  (Q&A), 91–92
Audience curiosity, 73–74
Audience expertise, honoring (Q&A),
  29–30
Audience feedback, 103, 105
  See also Evaluations
Audience knowledge,
  acknowledging, 28
Audience motivation (Q&A), 40–41
Audience participation. *See* Active
  participation, ensuring (Q&A)
Audience rapport, building, 27–28
Audience receptiveness, 74–75
Audience reviews. *See* Reviews
Audience's point of view (Q&A),
  30–31
Auditoriums, success in, 21, 22

Awards and prizes (Q&A), 80
Awareness of session gains (Q&A),
    91–92

Background articles, 7
Bag 'O Jokes (energizer), 61*f*
Barlett, J., 26
Barth, R., 55
Berra, Y., 57
Blaydes, J., 3, 17, 39, 42,
    44, 54, 57, 104
Bluffers, 75
Body communication, 34–35, 45
    See also Nonverbal communication
        (Q&A)
Book resources, sharing (Q&A), 14
Bower, B., 45
Brainstorming, variations on, 42, 97
Breakfast essentials, 10–11
Breaks (Q&A), 62
    See also Audience acceptance;
        Presenter technique; Reviews
Brink, S., 10
Burkman, M. A., 10

Carousel process, 24, 25n
Carper, J., 10
CD presentations, 14, 19
Chairs and tables, arranging, 21–23
    See also Facility setup
Changes of state (Q&A), 58–59
Charts, slides, and overheads (Q&A),
    23–24
    See also Presenter technique
Classroom-style room setups, 18*f*
Closure applications
    audience awareness of session gains
        (Q&A), 91–92
    do's and don'ts, 101
    lasting impressions and, 89–90
    positive endings (Q&A), 97–99,
        99*f*, 100*f*
    review, rehearsal, and application
        (Q&A), 92–97, 93*f*, 95*f*
    three features of quality closer
        (Q&A), 90–91
Collegial feedback (Q&A), 108–110

Color Disk Review (activity), 100*f*
Comfort, dressing for, 11
Comfort board (display), 78*f*
Comfort factors, 73
    See also Reviews
Common ground, establishing, 27,
    30–31
Commonalties, identifying,
    27, 30–31
Communication, exceeding
    expectations for, 3–5
    See also Preparation success
Communication, nonlinguistic, 45–46
Communication, nonverbal (Q&A),
    44–47
Communication, positive (Q&A),
    34–35
Complex issues, working with, 73
Computer setup, 19
Connections and reflections (Q&A),
    39–40
    See also Closure applications;
        Presenter technique
Consistency, an allusive target,
    102–103
Content, applying (Q&A), 69
Content, covering volumes of (Q&A),
    63–66, 64*f*
Content, limiting (Q&A), 39
Content, reinforcing, 40
Controversial questions, handling, 70
Covey, S., 17
Criticism, 106
Crowded seating, 23
Crutches to stay calm (Q&A), 20
Curiosity, audience, 73–74

Defensiveness, defusing, 29
Delays, legitimate, 25
Delivery process. *See* Presenter
    technique
Departures, audience, 101
Depression and sleep, 10
Difficult audiences, handling (Q&A),
    83–85
Directing attention (Q&A), 69
Directions, ensuring success to, 51

Disorganization. *See* Organization and
   time (Q&A)
Diuretics, eliminating, 15–16
Do's and don'ts, for
   audience acceptance, 35–36
   closure applications, 101
   enthusiasm and style, 70–71
   evaluations, 110
   facility setup, 25
   preparation essentials, 16
   preparation success, 8
   presenter technique, 52–53
   reviews, 88
Dressing for success, 11
Dry throat, 15

E-mail communication, 4–5
Eating essentials, 10–11
Electric plug adapter, 13
Emotional and physical comfort,
   creating (Q&A), 78–80
Emotional delivery. *See* Audience
   acceptance; Presenter technique
Emotional issues, dealing with, 86
Endings, positive (Q&A),
   97–99, 99*f,* 100*f*
See also Closure applications
Energizers (Q&A), 60, 61*f*
See also Enthusiasm and style
Energy, eating for sustained, 10–11
Enthusiasm and style
   1-2-3 rule, 57
   accountability in group work
      (Q&A), 66–67
   applying content (Q&A), 69
   breaks (Q&A), 62
   change of state (Q&A), 58–59
   covering volumes of content
      (Q&A), 63–66, 64*f*
   directing attention (Q&A), 69
   do's and don'ts, 70–71
   energizers (Q&A), 60, 61*f*
   group size (Q&A), 67
   handling questions (Q&A),
      69–70
   infusing excitement into sessions,
      54–55

introductions set the tone (Q&A),
      57–58
   lecturing (Q&A), 62–63
   monitoring an audience, 55–57
   movement (Q&A), 59–60
   participation energy level, 56*f*
   personality and, 54
   variety as a vehicle, 55
   visuals to enhance meaning (Q&A),
      67–69, 68*f*
Entrances (Q&A), 24–25
See also Facility setup
Equipment trouble, heading off
   (Q&A), 14–15
Evaluations
   collegial feedback (Q&A),
      108–110
   consistency an allusive target,
      102–103
   do's and don'ts, 110
   formal feedback (Q&A), 105–107
   informal feedback (Q&A), 104–105
   inviting improvement, 103–104
   Secrets to Success, 103, 110n
Event files, maintaining, 4, 5
Excitement, infusing into sessions,
      54–55
Expectations, exceeding, 3–4, 32
Expertise, honoring audience (Q&A),
      29–30
Extroverts, 84
Eye contact, 34, 57

Facial communication, 34–35, 45
See also Nonverbal communication
   (Q&A)
Facility assessments, 17
Facility setup
   charts, slides, and overheads,
      23–24
   crutches to stay calm (Q&A), 20
   distributing handouts/materials, 23
   do's and don'ts, 25
   grand entrances (Q&A), 24–25
   materials, 19
   readying the facility, 17
   room setup (Q&A), 21

room setup types, 18*f*
seating participants (Q&A), 21–23
start before you begin, 19–20
Fahey, J. A., 15
Familiarity, realm of, 27
Feedback, participant, 103, 105
See also Evaluations
15-minute welcome, 19–20, 24–25
Finesse factors, 74–75
First client contact, 3–4
Fluid consumption (Q&A), 15–16
Follow-up calls, 5
Formal feedback (Q&A), 105–107
Friendliness, realm of, 27–28
Fun factors, 72–73
See also Reviews

Gandhi, M., 37
Gardner, H., 44
Glare, overhead, 15
Greeting participants, 19–20, 24–25
Group energy *vs.* group scatter, 22
Group size (Q&A), 67
Group work, accountability in (Q&A), 66–67
Group work, rules for, 52
Gutin, J. C., 1

Half round room setups, 18*f*, 21
Handouts, distributing (Q&A), 23
Handouts, preparing (Q&A), 6–7
Happiness, in presentation, 72–73
Hard-to-reach clients, 5
Herringbone room setups, 18*f*
Humility (Q&A), 85–86
Humor, using, 44, 73, 77, 97–98
Hydration essentials (Q&A), 15–16

Illumination distractions, 15
Illustrations and stories, using, 31
Impressions, lasting, 89–90
Improvement, inviting, 103–104, 107
Individual tally task, 95–96
Informal feedback (Q&A), 104–105
Information, skills, and message (Q&A), 38–39
Interactions, before session, 19–20, 24–25

Interruptions, 70
Introductions, set the tone (Q&A), 57–58
Introductions and openers (Q&A), 32–34, 33*f*
Involvement, maintaining (Q&A), 48–49
See also Presenter technique

Jigsaw format, 65, 66
Jones, S., 3, 89, 105, 110

Keynote addresses, 63
See also specific topics
King, D., 39
Klein, A., 44
Knowledge and know-how, acknowledging, 28

Laser pointers, 13
Last minute preparation. *See* Preparation essentials
Lasting impressions, 89–90
Late arrivals, legitimate, 25
Lead-up time, 19–20
Learning, building fun into (Q&A), 75–77
Lecturing (Q&A), 62–63
Lincoln, A., 9

Marzano, R. J., 67
Masking tape, 12
Materials, distributing (Q&A), 23
Materials, packing, 12–13
Materials, setting up, 19
Mehrabian, A., 45
Memorization, of presentation, 8, 20
Message, information, and skills (Q&A), 38–39
Metaphors, effectiveness of, 43–44
Microphone positioning, 24
Misunderstanding, minimizing chance for (Q&A), 4–5
See also Presenter technique
Mixers, meaningful (Q&A), 80–81, 81*f*
See also Reviews
Monitoring an audience, 55–57

Monotony, 54–55, 59
Morning sessions, 9–10
Motivating an audience (Q&A), 40–41
Movement (Q&A), 59–60
    See also Reviews
Music, using, 19, 35, 62, 76, 77
Mystery factors, 73–74

National Sleep Foundation, 10
Negative evaluations, 106
    See also Evaluations
Nonlinguistic communication, 45–46
Nonverbal communication (Q&A),
    44–47
    See also Presenter technique
Note-cards, presenter, 20
Note-taking, considerations for, 7

Observer critiques, 103, 108–110
1-2-3 rule, 57
Openers and introductions (Q&A),
    32–34, 33*f*
Organization and time (Q&A),
    82–83
    See also Preparation success
Organizing for relaxed delivery
    (Q&A), 8
Overflow crowd, seating, 22
Overhead glare, 15
Overheads, charts, and slides (Q&A),
    23–24
    See also Presenter technique
Overviews and agendas (Q&A),
    31–32

Packing checklist (Q&A), 12–13
Packing essentials, 11–12
Pair Reading (technique), 64*f*
Parameters. *See* Tight parameters,
    to ensure success (Q&A)
Participation. *See* Presenter technique
Participation energy level, 56*f*
Peale, N. V., 104
Peer reporting, 29
Peer Sharing (energizer), 61*f*
People Shuffle (mixer), 81*f*
Peoples, D., 45
Performers *vs.* presenters, 8

Personal quirks, working around,
    28–29
Personal shortcomings, working
    around, 28–29
Personal stories, using, 31
Personality, 54
Phone conversations, 4–5
Physical and emotional comfort,
    creating (Q&A), 78–80
Physical Movement (energizer), 61*f*
    See also Movement (Q&A)
Pickering, D. J., 67
Pike, R. W., 66
Podiums, 30, 39
Point of view, changing audience's
    (Q&A), 30–31
Pointers, presentation, 13
Pollock, J. E., 67
Positive communication (Q&A),
    34–35
Postsession evaluations, 40
    See also Evaluations
Posture, 34
PowerPoint presentations, 14
Preparation essentials
    do's and don'ts, 16
    dressing for success, 11
    eating for sustained energy,
        10–11
    heading off equipment trouble
        (Q&A), 14–15
    hydration (Q&A), 15–16
    packing checklist (Q&A), 12–13
    packing light, 11–12
    sharing book resources (Q&A), 14
    sleep for efficiency, 9–10
Preparation of facility. *See* Facility
    setup
Preparation success
    clear communication and, 3–4
    do's and don'ts, 8
    minimizing chance for
        misunderstanding (Q&A), 4–5
    organizing for relaxed delivery
        (Q&A), 8
    preparing handouts (Q&A), 6–7
    tailoring programs (Q&A), 6
Presentation memorization, 8, 20

Presentation requests, filling, 5
See also Preparation success
Presenter technique
 do's and don'ts, 52–53
 ensuring active participation
  (Q&A), 49–50
 generating new thinking (Q&A), 42
 information, skills, and message
  (Q&A), 38–39
 limiting content (Q&A), 39
 maintaining involvement (Q&A),
  48–49
 motivating an audience (Q&A),
  40–41
 nonverbal communication (Q&A),
  44–47
 purpose drives process, 37–38
 reflections and connections (Q&A),
  39–40
 regaining attention (Q&A), 49
 small groups to enliven learning
  (Q&A), 47–48
 tight parameters to ensure success
  (Q&A), 51–52
 timing group work (Q&A), 48
 understanding (Q&A), 42–44
Presenting, effectiveness of, 1–2
Prizes and awards (Q&A), 80
Professional observers, 103, 108–110
Professional supplies, packing, 12–13
See also Preparation essentials
Project files, maintaining, 4, 5
Projection devices, 14, 17
Purpose, drives process, 37–38
See also Presenter technique

Quality closure, three features of
 (Q&A), 90–91
Questions, handling (Q&A), 69–70
See also Reviews
Quirks, working around, 28
Quotation Center, 44
Quotes, ending, 97

Random selection, 49, 50
Rapport, building audience, 27–28
Read, Reflect, Respond
 (technique), 64*f*

Receptiveness, audience, 74–75
Rectangular shaped room setups, 18*f*
Reflections and connections (Q&A),
 39–40
See also Closure applications;
  Presenter technique
Rehearsal, application and review
 (Q&A), 92–97, 93*f,* 95*f*
Resistance, to training, 84
Review, rehearsal, and application
 (Q&A), 92–97, 93*f,* 95*f*
Reviews
 building fun into learning (Q&A),
  75–77
 comfort factors, 73
 creating physical and emotional
  comfort (Q&A), 78–80
 do's and don'ts, 88
 finesse factors, 74–75
 fun factors, 72–73
 handling difficult audiences (Q&A),
  83–85
 humility (Q&A), 85–86
 meaningful mixers (Q&A), 80–81,
  81*f*
 mystery factors, 73–74
 presenter appeal and, 72
 prizes and awards (Q&A), 80
 setting yourself apart (Q&A),
  86–88
 time and organization (Q&A),
  82–83
 when you don't have the answer
  (Q&A), 75
Room assessments, 17
Room setup (Q&A), 21
Room setup types, 18*f*

Scissors, storing, 13
Seating participants (Q&A), 21–23
Secrets to Success, 103, 110n
Self-evaluations, 34, 105
See also Evaluations
Selsor, K., 40
Sequenced Circle Review (task), 93*f*
Session delays, legitimate, 25
Setting yourself apart (Q&A), 86–88
Setup preparation. *See* Facility setup

Shero, F., 54
Shoe essentials, 11
Shortcomings, working around, 28–29
Skills, message, and information
     (Q&A), 38–39
Sleep, for efficiency, 9–10
Slides, charts, and overheads (Q&A),
     23–24
     See also Preparation success;
          Presenter technique
Small groups, to enliven learning
     (Q&A), 47–48
Space considerations. *See* Facility
     setup
Stand Up If (energizer), 61*f*
Stimulation, as vehicle, 55
Stories and illustrations, using, 31
Streng, K., 10
Style. *See* Enthusiasm and style
Supplies, packing, 12–13
Supplies, setting up, 19

T-I-E (Time, Interaction, and Energy),
     59, 66
Tables and chairs, arranging, 21–23
     See also Facility setup
Tailoring programs (Q&A), 6
Team building, 32
Technique. *See* Presenter technique
Theater-style room setups, 18*f*, 21
Thinking, generating new (Q&A), 42
Three Card Toss (activity), 98–99
Tight parameters, to ensure success
     (Q&A), 51–52
Time and organization (Q&A), 82–83
     See also Presenter technique

Timing group work (Q&A), 48
Tomasino, C., 108
Toothbrush, 12
Transitions, 59
Transparencies, using, 15, 20, 24
Travel clock, 13
Travel preparation. *See* Preparation
     essentials
Travel wet cloths, 12
Traveling cards, 75

U-shaped room setups, 18*f*
Understanding (Q&A), 42–44
     See also Presenter technique

Van Cautier, E., 10
Variety, as a vehicle, 55
Verbal contracts, 4–5
Videotaping, 34–35
Vis-à-Vis pens, 19
Visibility, increasing (Q&A), 30
Visiting, before session,
     19–20, 24–25
Visual distractions, 15
Visuals, to enhance meaning (Q&A),
     67–69, 68*f*
     See also Presenter technique
Voice, 55
Volunteer selection, 49, 50
Vulnerability, 27, 29–30

Winfrey, O., 3
Wolfe, P., 10, 73
Word choice, 44–45
Write-on transparencies, 13, 19
     See also Transparencies, using

**CORWIN
PRESS**

The Corwin Press logo—a raven striding across an open book—represents the union of courage and learning. Corwin Press is committed to improving education for all learners by publishing books and other professional development resources for those serving the field of PreK–12 education. By providing practical, hands-on materials, Corwin Press continues to carry out the promise of its motto: **"Helping Educators Do Their Work Better."**

Printed in the United States
By Bookmasters